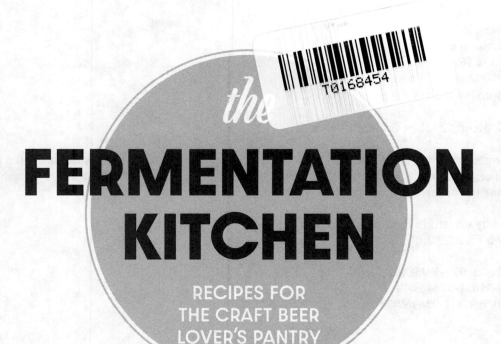

the FERMENTATION KITCHEN

RECIPES FOR THE CRAFT BEER LOVER'S PANTRY

BY GABE TOTH

BREWERS PUBLICATIONS.

Brewers Publications®
A Division of the Brewers Association
PO Box 1679, Boulder, Colorado 80306-1679
BrewersAssociation.org
BrewersPublications.com

Proudly Printed in the United States of America.
10 9 8 7 6 5 4 3 2 1

ISBN-13: 978-1-938469-71-8
ISBN-10: 1-938469-71-2
EISBN: 978-1-938469-72-5

Library of Congress Control Number: 2021940808

Publisher: Kristi Switzer
Technical Editor: Lorena Evans
Copyediting: Iain Cox
Indexing: Doug Easton
Art Direction, Interior Design, Production: Jason Smith
Cover Photo: Souders Studios
Interior photos by Gabe Toth unless specified otherwise.

This book is for those with an insatiable urge to create, taste, and explore.

offering samples and then suddenly back out, cautiously uttering excuses as to why they wanted no part of trying the foods. I always joked we were selling the country cousin to the more popular fermented foods, like artisan cheeses, sourdough breads, and, of course, wine and beer. Slowly, though, people became interested and curious. They wanted to know more and understand these foods. What I didn't know, nor fully understand at the time, was that in the seemingly innocuous act of fermenting food ourselves we were part of a small grassroots revolution. The rebellion was simply eating well—good, whole, real food— by allowing microbes back into our kitchens, not as something to be feared and doused in antibacterial products but as helpers, or tiny chefs, in our food preparation. It can feel like a radical act against the status quo.

My story with fermentation begins at the end of the last century when we bought a small piece of land and began growing our own food. When you produce food, you can quickly have too much of one thing to consume before it goes bad. Thus begins the quest to preserve. For our family this began when our son wanted to raise dairy goats, which almost immediately resulted in more milk than we could keep up with. We quickly turned to fermentation, first yogurt, then soft fresh cheeses, feta pickling in brine, and finally hard cheese wheels aging in our makeshift cheese "cave." The "old-timers" around us were retirees from a modern era of professional jobs and commodified food, not people that knew how to make cheese using milk fresh from a cow. We had the one cheesemaking book available (and it was lacking) and cheesemaking wasn't a Google search away. Many mistakes, punctuated by just enough delicious successes, went into teaching ourselves how to shepherd the desired microbes into this most magical of fermentation transformations—cheese.

As we grew more food and our fermentation-as-preservation skills expanded (by necessity), I became challenged, maybe even a little obsessed, with the idea of serving meals where everything on the plate had been produced on our small holding. When the oak farmhouse table was laden with fermented asparagus spears, cultured butter, fresh cheese melted over au gratin potatoes dug from the earth of our garden, fried eggs, and fresh salad dressed with homemade apple cider vinegar, seeing this bounty that our hands and the fermenting microbes had produced was deeply satisfying for me. This unrealistic, idealistic passion has long faded. Over the ensuing decades our children grew and grew and grew up. Our homestead downsized to smaller gardens and my desire to help folks embrace these foods over the next decade became five books covering some of the comestibles in this wide-reaching craft. But as I read *The Fermentation Kitchen: Recipes for the Craft Beer Lover's Pantry* I was reminded of that early time. In one book Gabe Toth deftly sets the bounty to be enjoyed on the table. (Don't worry, Gabe doesn't expect you to grow any of your food.) You are invited into Gabe's kitchen. He makes accessible the skills for exploring and connecting with food crafts that make a life worth living. His book is a welcome addition to the small but growing canon of fermentation works.

It was a hot Colorado summer day when I met Gabe at a corner coffee shop. We sat at a table under a shade tree, sipping tea and talking about fermentation. We talked about Colorado's grain growers, small growers using regenerative principles, independent craft maltsters, and the systems that feed Colorado's brewing and distilling industry. Gabe is passionate about supply chain localization, sustainability, and terroir. He has structured his world to reimagine and reinvent the structures within brewing and distilling supply chains through his work as a head distiller and as a writer and editor for the industry. I was struck by his energy and curiosity around food systems and fermentation. When I asked him, "Why this book?" Gabe answered that, instead of a book on a single subject, he wanted a book that would give people a tour of what was possible with fermentation and the knowledge to do so safely. His feeling, which is apparent as you read the book, is that if you have the structure and the rules, you will know which dials you can turn to create ferments that are uniquely yours.

It is clear that Gabe's years of home fermenting stand behind the recipes in this book. Well researched, the techniques are presented with clear information on the microbes that are responsible for each of the fermentations. He weaves history and science into the understanding of these foods. To this end, Gabe tackles salt in an appendix to help the reader understand this often-maligned ingredient. Salt has moved armies because of its importance to our very existence. Gabe's on-point discussion is an important part of the larger conversation around sodium chloride.

Each chapter takes you on a journey of understanding that leads you to recipes so that you can eventually revel in their making, be it pulling fat pretzels from your oven, delighting over the carbonation of your own homemade flavored kombucha, smelling the acidity develop in a fruit vinegar, hanging cheesecloth-swathed yogurt over a bowl to become *labneh*, or thinly slicing your own lardo to wrap around pieces of cool, sweet cantaloupe. As you read, Gabe invites you to begin your journey in fermented foods wherever you want: crusty bread or sourdough *boules* straight from the oven, fermented relishes and pickles, creamy cheese, fermented mustards, or cured meats. And, if you end up doing all these things, you will find that you fermented all the parts of an epic charcuterie board. That's when it's time to invite over your friends and celebrate!

Kirsten K. Shockey
Author of *Homebrewed Vinegar*;
coauthor of the award-winning books
*The Big Book of Cidermaking and Miso,
Tempeh, Natto & Other Tasty Ferments*;
Fiery Ferments; and the best-selling
Fermented Vegetables

ACKNOWLEDGMENTS

As with all endeavors, the writing of this book did not occur in a void. We all stand on the shoulders of giants, and I owe a great well of gratitude and thanks to so many people.

To all of the cooks, authors, and artisans whose work this book relies on. Some are listed in the bibliography. Countless others have developed the common knowledge that underlies most of this book, or made a dish that inspired a recipe or flavor combination.

To my wife, Stefanie Page, who continued to be supportive of this project even when it meant that I spent late nights and long weekends locked in the basement writing. And even when it meant there were piles of bread and cheese around the house that had to be eaten.

To my parents, who taught me and my brothers the difference between real food and junk food.

To the countless friends and coworkers who have tasted these recipes over the years, offering ideas, critical input, and encouragement.

Thank you all, from the bottom of my heart.

Finally, 2020 was a year that we could never forget. Far too many friends and mentors who were around when this work was started did not get to see it finished. Michael Johnstone and George Medina, Patience Robinson-Campos, Professor Richard Joyce, and dear old Bear, you will never be forgotten.

INTRODUCTION

Fermentation, whether applied to vegetables, meat, grain, or a wide variety of other ingredients, is a fundamental force in the human experience. It is a part of us. The microbiological organisms that drive fermentation processes—fungi, like yeast and mold, and bacteria—are embedded in our culture and our biology. They existed long before we learned to harness them in even the most rudimentary way, and human civilization has evolved in the constant presence of fermented food and drink. It could even be argued that fermentation helped to drive the start of early agricultural civilization. Academics may differ on whether bread or beer impelled early humans to settle down and begin growing grain, but the choice is between one fermented food or another, that is, bread or liquid bread.

An estimated one-third of the food that humans eat every day is fermented. This includes breads, cured or semicured sausages, traditional pickles like sauerkraut, and Asian staples such as miso and fish sauce. Coffee beans are fermented when fresh. The pulp of cacao beans is also fermented, allowing for the conversion of bitter phenolic compounds to less bitter compounds and enabling the breakdown of proteins into simple amino acids and sugars. The cacao fermentation process brings about a remarkable change, converting what were tasteless, astringent beans into "vessels laden with desirable flavors and flavor precursors," yielding flavors of fruit and wine, sugars, complex acids, and floral notes (McGee 2004, 698).

Even the much-maligned monosodium glutamate (MSG) is a product of fermentation. It is the naturally occurring salt of the amino acid glutamate, and provides a savory kick to foods such as tomatoes, Parmesan cheese, and meat. Originally isolated from Japanese seaweed (*kombu*) broth, MSG is now created by fermenting starch and sugars.[1]

Unfortunately, the commodification of food as part of its industrialization over the last century has led to a reduction in the types of fermented foods and processes used to create them. This book is not intended as a polemic; it is not a manifesto or an in-depth examination of the harmful trends in our food culture. Nonetheless, it is impossible to ignore the broader world in which this work is being composed. The remainder of this book will focus on fermentation principles, techniques, ingredients, and recipes. But for just a moment, let us step back and put food fermentation in context.

I, like so many others, grew up in the general environment of industrial food production that has transformed our food systems over the last century. Forty years old at the time of this publication, I have witnessed firsthand the generation-to-generation decline of home cooking, from being a part of the daily routine to now being an occasional experience. I have encouraged countless friends and coworkers over the years to learn the basics of how to cook their own food. I know that my peers and their children are eating less and less home-made food and more and more processed, prepackaged, or restaurant-made food.

It is impossible to separate the cultural and dietary impacts of the increasing disconnect between food producers and consumers from other changes in the way we live that have happened over the last century. The post-WWII industrialization of food, which has leaned heavily on fat, salt, sugar, and novel chemicals, can certainly be credited as a contributor to the current obesity crisis and its related illnesses. Michael Pollan (2013, 8) has commented on the substantial toll industrial cooking has had on our health and well-being, adding that "corporations cook very differently from how people do (which is why we usually call what they do 'food processing' instead of cooking)."

It is not a black-and-white question of home-cooked food versus fast food. Few people live exclusively in either one of these places, but as a whole we are moving farther from the production side of our food. This disengagement from the source of our food and the processes that turn ingredients into food changes the way we understand food. The commodification of food has rendered it an abstraction. "Indeed," writes Pollan, "the idea that food has any connection to nature or human work or imagination is hard to credit when it arrives in a neat package, fully formed" (2013, 9).

I have experienced this mindset in person, the first time a friend and I raised pigs. We invited the production staff at the brewery where we both worked to come out and help with the slaughter and butchery of four pigs (a considerable undertaking without extra hands). Several coworkers were excited about taking part, while others were explicit in their preference to stay at arm's length. "My meat comes in styrofoam trays," one of them told me. Willful ignorance, the result of which, if taken to its logical conclusion, creates the very real possibility that "within another generation, cooking a meal from scratch will seem as exotic and ambitious—as 'extreme'—as most of us today regard brewing beer or baking a loaf of bread or putting up a crock of sauerkraut" (Pollan 2013, 17).

It is also possible that the economic hangover of a worldwide pandemic, paired with a changed approach to life prompted by more than a year of social distancing, proves these words false. To view the industrialization of food as inevitably continuing into the future is to ignore small but heartening trends.

In recent decades, the pendulum has begun to swing, very slowly and incrementally, back in the other direction. There is excitement around healthy dining, as well as around the economic benefits of preparing food at home and the satisfaction to be had from creating quality home-fermented foods. Diners are

---

[1] "Questions and Answers on Monosodium Glutamate (MSG)," U.S. Food and Drug Administration, November 19, 2012, https://www.fda.gov/food/food-additives-petitions/questions-and-answers-monosodium-glutamate-msg.

also looking for farm-to-table restaurants; farmers, millers, and bakers are creating local grain economies; and small fermented-food businesses have begun to spring up, offering pickles, sauerkraut, and other local products, first at farmers markets, then at small local or regional grocers, and in some cases now at national chains. A small cross-section of consumers is beginning to recognize that food is a part of a much wider agricultural web that includes farmers, microbes, and healthy soil.

Sandor Katz helped to kick-start the home-fermentation revival in the United States with the publication of his groundbreaking book *Wild Fermentation* in 2003, following it nine years later with the encyclopedic *Art of Fermentation*. The food movement that Katz has come to personify pushes against the modern move towards increasing specialization. Reconnecting with the source of your food is educational, even enlightening, and encourages a greater sense of responsibility for your place in the food chain.

Ferments are among the original value-added products, in which the raw outputs of agriculture are transformed, via great technique and artistry, into delicacies that are stable and can be transported, and that fill our kitchens and food stores. . . . The revival of fermentation at the local and regional scale goes hand in hand with the revival of local agriculture in the movement toward relocalization of our food and our economics. (Katz 2012, 369)

Michael Pollan (2013, 407) has developed this theme further, describing a transition from a food system in which we are simply consumers, passive recipients who are kept ignorant about the origins of what we consume, to one where we are elevated to partners in the food web.

My own journey into fermentation began in 2005 with homebrewing. I had heard stories about my parents making dandelion wine, so creating booze always seemed nebulous but within reach. I had a roommate my last year of college who had homebrewed and talked about how we could certainly do it in our apartment (though we never did). It was Colorado in the early 2000s, so this roommate turned me

to craft beer and high-quality German beers and I never looked back. Within a year of graduating, I was making my own homebrew of questionable quality. A year or two later I started looking at the seasonal bounty at the grocery store: I saw how a given crop would be available in great mounds for low prices at certain times of the year, and I wondered how to take advantage of that. I always loved strong, sharp flavors like vinegar and salt, and decided it was time to start learning how to pickle vegetables.

Vinegar and salt—strong flavors like this have always enticed me. As a kid, once I was old enough to get on my bike and go on adventures through suburban New Jersey, I loved stopping at Wawa for an Italian sandwich piled high with cured meats. And I always got one of those extra-vinegary pickles from the plastic barrel they had at the deli.

A friend in college who was half Japanese and half Samoan first introduced me to kimchi, which he described at the time as "rotting cabbage." Eventually, I found a Korean grocer in town where I could buy kimchi by the gallon and so I often kept it on hand. One year, when I was still spending summer and winter breaks at my parents' house, I picked up a jar at the end of the semester to tide me over until I went back to school. My dad took one sniff and forbade me from bringing home kimchi ever again.

Pickling turned to cheesemaking, which led in turn to cured meat and, once there was some yard space, a garden was in order. Eventually, raising pigs and chickens became part of the rotation. Almost 20 years later, my wife and I visited my parents and I let them know I had brought some meats, cheeses, and pickles. Dad asked, "But no kimchi, right?" I laughed and confirmed that was right. It had made an impression on him, that was for sure.

I do not consider myself an expert in the fermenting arts, but I have been fine-tuning these methods for years, almost 15 years in some cases. More than anything, I am a student. While this book was written with both brewers and homebrewers in mind—who may have a head start on understanding the process of fermentation and an appropriate view of microbiological culture as omnipresent—it is also meant for the general aficionado

1

ABOUT
FERMENTATION METHODS

Broadly speaking, the practice of fermentation is a collection of methods and techniques that harness microbial life to transform and preserve food. Prior to the advent of refrigeration and modern chemical preservatives, fermentation was used so that humans could continue to make use of food long after it was harvested, the preserved remains of summer and fall crops often carrying people through the harsh winter.

The practice of fermentation, in its various forms, spans the globe. Fermentation may be a uniquely ubiquitous form of food preparation, accounting for as much as a third of the world's diet. It is seemingly a universal facet of humanity; there is no culture that does not practice some fermentation of food or drink, and even in modern industrialized societies it remains one of the most important ways that food is processed (Pollan 2013, 303).

THE WELLNESS TREND

Fermented foods can be beneficial for our health. The fermentation process enzymatically breaks down nutrients that we would otherwise be unable to digest, increasing the bioavailability of these nutrients. These enzymatic processes also produce crucial vitamins. Thus, fermentation increases the amount of vitamin C (ascorbic acid) and B vitamins available in vegetables, including folic acid, riboflavin, niacin, thiamin, and biotin; creates B_{12}, which does not naturally occur in vegetables, and vitamin K; makes iron more soluble; and even increases the stimulating properties of tea (this is why black and oolong teas are more potent than green tea.) The process of fermentation increases the vitamin C content of sauerkraut to 400% more than the plain cabbage from which it was created.[1]

There is a lot of talk these days about "gut health" and the gut microbiome being beneficial to people's overall health. Because probiotics are known to be created by fermentation, this has created a craze and boosted the number of people who are trying home fermentation. Restaurant consumption of fermented foods went up an astounding 149% in 2018.[2] The wellness trend continued through 2019 and even more people began fermenting at home during the pandemic in 2020.

After humanity discovered agriculture, the human diet narrowed dramatically to a few starchy staples: rice, wheat, corn, and potatoes. Intensely flavored fermented foods allowed people to spice up an otherwise uninteresting meal while also supplying much-needed nutrients. Compare the flavors in the products of modern food production—canned food, soy-based "meats," artificial sweeteners, and high-fructose corn syrup—with those in cheese, wine and beer, chocolate, soy sauce, coffee, yogurt, cured olives, vinegar, pickled vegetables, and cured meats. Even after millennia of producing our own food rather than foraging for it, "we still haven't discovered techniques for processed food as powerful, versatile, safe, or nutritious as microbial fermentation" (Pollan 2013, 310).

Fermented foods can evoke strong responses though. One culture's delicacy, perhaps a moldy cheese or a well-aged kimchi, can be extremely unpleasant to someone unaccustomed to those flavors and aromas. Fermentation sometimes hugs the line between fermented and rotten, a very subjective boundary that is often defined culturally. Our innate aversion to signs of decay in food is a natural—even reasonable—evolutionary trait, but one that can cause a person to miss out on unique, delicious, and safe food experiences.

> "
>
> *Between fresh and rotten,*
>
> *there is a creative space in which*
>
> *some of the most compelling*
>
> *of flavors arise.*
>
> — Sandor Katz,
> *The Art of Fermentation*, p. 35

Fundamentally, the process of fermenting food takes advantage of the broader microbial environment. While some common fermentations, such as beer making, occur in a relatively sanitary environment that promotes a cultured microbe added to perform a specific task, fermentations rarely occur in such a biological void. To effectively ferment food, you can harness factors such as salt, acidity, lack of water, and lack of oxygen to favor the desired microbial activity, while undesired microbes are crowded out or unable to grow in such a hostile high-salinity, low-pH, low-moisture, and/or anaerobic environment. Manipulating conditions like this need not be complicated. Something as simple as submerging cabbage under brine to act as a barrier to air and oxygen yields sauerkraut "rather than a puddle of slime" (Katz 2012, 38).

YEASTS, MOLDS, AND BACTERIA

Food fermentation deals primarily with three classes of microbes: yeasts, molds, and bacteria. In different circumstances, there are populations of all three that can transform your food and elevate it, and other populations that can ruin it. Yeasts and molds are both fungi that can transform your food but they are also very different microbes. Yeast can grow both aerobically (in the presence of free oxygen) and anaerobically (in the absence of free oxygen), but mold can only grow aerobically. Yeast are single-celled organisms that produce asexually

---

[1] O.K. Chun, N. Smith, A. Sakagawa, and C.Y. Lee, "Antioxidant Properties of Raw and Processed Cabbages," *International Journal of Food Sciences and Nutrition* 55, no. 3 (May 2004): 191–199, https://doi.org/10.1080/09637480410001725148.

[2] Lizzy Saxe, "Fermented Foods Are Up 149% – As Long As They're Unfamiliar," Food and Drink, *Forbes*, February 6, 2019, 10:07 a.m. EST, https://www.forbes.com/sites/lizzysaxe/2019/02/06/fermented-foods-are-up-149-percent-as-long-as-theyre-unfamiliar/.

by fission or budding, whereas molds are multicellular and reproduce sexually or asexually.

Bacteria are our primary concern when it comes to pathogenic dangers; this includes *Listeria monocytogenes* (the cause of listeriosis), *Escherichia coli* (E. coli O157:H7 poisoning), *Staphylococcus aureus* (staph infections), and *Clostridium botulinum* (botulism), among others. Most bacteria are aerobic (requiring oxygen) and most are dormant at low temperatures. They are most active in what the USDA calls the "danger zone," a temperature range from 40°F to 140°F (4–60°C). To be safe, remember that below 40°F (4°C) many bacteria will slow and stop reproducing, and above 140°F (60°C) many will begin to die; however, there are many species that will remain active and viable outside of this temperature range. Some, such as *C. botulinum*, will create spores that can survive temperatures above boiling (see "Botulism" sidebar on p. 10).

When the proper methods are used on uncontaminated ingredients, fermented foods are generally considered safe. These methods evolved over thousands of years to provide preserved and nourishing food. Foods do not usually reach an optimal point of safety based on one factor (i.e., only salt, dehydration, or acidity), so most fermentation methods operate on the concept that each individual factor is detrimental to the bacterial population and therefore a combination of factors can act as a tag team to fight pathogenic bacteria and help keep food safe.

Different types of fermented foods rely on different factors or combinations of factors to maintain safety. Salt is such a fundamental factor in food preservation and fermentation that it is used in almost every recipe in this book.

Working hand-in-hand with salt, acidification is a widely used approach that can be found in various forms of fermented vegetables (pickled vegetables, hot sauces, relishes, etc.), semicured fermented sausages, cheese, kombucha, and vinegar. Acidity in a product is reflected in the food or drink's pH level. A measure of the concentration of available hydrogen ions, pH is short for "potential of hydrogen" and is measured on a scale that typically runs from zero to 14.0. (In extreme circumstances, values below zero and above 14.0 can be reached, but such solutions would be so highly corrosive that they are of no use for food production.) Pure water is neutral with a pH of 7.0; a pH above that is alkaline (e.g., baking soda, soap, bleach, and lye), and a pH below that is acidic. It should be noted that the pH scale is logarithmic. This means that a drop from a pH of 5.0 to a pH of 4.0 means a ten-fold increase in acidity. Likewise, going from pH 5.0 to pH 3.0 indicates a hundred times more acidity.

Many foods tend to be in the range of pH 5.0 to 7.0, which is right where bacteria will thrive. Below pH 5.0 the environment is more inhospitable for bacteria. Most finished beers have a pH of a little over 4.0, fermented pickles can drop to 3.0, white vinegar is 2.0 to 2.5, lemon juice is about 2.0, and a solution of hydrochloric acid can reach zero.

Lowering the pH of food is a sound way to eliminate pathogenic bacteria. *C. botulinum* will not grow below pH 5.0, while the viability of many others (e.g., *Staphylococcus*, *Campylobacter*, *Listeria*, and *Escherichia* species) falls off between 4.0 and 5.0 in otherwise favorable conditions. Salmonella bacteria can hang on until pH 3.8 in otherwise favorable conditions.

Another aspect you can take advantage of, especially when producing cured meats, is water activity (a_w). This is a measure of the amount of water that is chemically available to react with (note that a_w is not an indication of how much water is in the product). The a_w of pure distilled water is 1.0, while the complete absence of moisture is an a_w of zero. For context on how much moisture must be removed to get to zero, consider that dried fruit still has an a_w of about 0.6; evaporated milk and instant coffee are still around 0.2. Even in food products that we may think are little more than dust, there are still trace levels of available moisture.

Hard cheeses and salamis, with an a_w of 0.85 or less, are generally at or near the USDA threshold for "potentially hazardous foods"—below that level is considered shelf-stable regardless of other factors. Almost all pathogenic bacteria, including listeria, *E. coli*, salmonella, and *C. botulinum*, are eliminated below an a_w of 0.91. *Staphylococcus aureus* can grow in environments with an a_w as low as 0.86.

Environments with higher levels of available water are more welcoming for pathogenic growth. Water activity can be lowered by binding up water with salt and sugar, by reducing the overall amount of water through drying, or both. Salt and sugar do not remove water from food, but they combine with it chemically and make it unavailable for use by microbes. However, there is a threshold where food becomes inedibly salty and a wide range where it is edible but unpleasantly salty, so salt must be used in combination with other methods. The practical implications of a_w and moisture loss will be discussed in more depth in the charcuterie chapter (pp. 135–136), where it is applied to fermented semicured sausages.

Maintaining an anaerobic environment is also critical for many fermentations, including fermented vegetables and the interiors of sausages and cheeses. Classically, fermentation was defined as an anaerobic process, but it is now used casually to describe any microbial transformation of food or drink. For example, any SCOBY, which is short for symbiotic culture of bacteria and yeast, that is responsible for the transformation of sweetened tea into kombucha contains both microbes that require oxygen (aerobes) and microbes that require a zero-oxygen environment (anaerobes). The SCOBY forms a cellulose mat at the surface of the liquid that serves as an intermediary between the atmosphere and anaerobes that make up the lower layers of the SCOBY. Vinegar production by species of the bacterial genus *Acetobacter* is another example of an aerobic process, where the microbial transformation requires oxygen to proceed.

Botulism

One notorious and potentially deadly anaerobe that we have to be extremely cautious of is *Clostridium botulinum*, the cause of botulism. Nowadays, botulism is associated with improperly canned foods (both homemade and commercial) and, more recently, with a series of consumers who were made ill after consuming olive oil infused with fresh garlic (Abo et al. 2014). However, botulism was originally associated with sausages, and even takes its name from the Latin *botulus*, or sausage, because primitive versions of sausages, prior to the understanding of nitrates and fermentation, provided an ideal environment for *C. botulinum* to thrive.

Botulism is a potentially fatal neurological disease that results from the botulinum toxin made by *C. botulinum* in low-acidity, anaerobic environments. The toxin acts on muscles and causes blurred vision or double vision, slurred speech, muscle weakness, and difficulty swallowing. (The toxin's ability to paralyze muscles has also been harnessed for cosmetic treatment under the name Botox.)

In America, a large percentage of the botulism cases that occur every year in adults are attributable to improper home-canning of low-acid foods (i.e., foods with a pH above 4.6) such as green beans, corn, potatoes, or meat. Because *C. botulinum* creates spores that can survive above 212°F (100°C), low-acid/low-salt foods must be pressure-cooked to fully destroy the spores and the bacteria.

C. botulinum is inhibited by acidity, reduced water activity, and sodium nitrate. Salt has a limited effect on the microbe's growth, so salt must be used in conjunction with sodium nitrate. It is important to remember that the toxin can remain even after the bacteria has died. For example, in a dry-cured sausage made without nitrate where *C. botulinum* was able to thrive initially but died off when the moisture level dropped or acidity level increased, the toxin is left behind and remains a significant threat to anyone who consumes the sausage.

Finally, neither the bacteria nor the toxin can be tasted. There are no flavor or aroma indicators to warn you that a food has been contaminated with the botulinum toxin or has *C. botulinum* growing in it. If you suspect that a food may not have been produced safely, it is always best to err on the side of caution and dispose of it.

The potential danger from *C. botulinum* and other pathogens should not deter you from fermenting food though. The solution is not to try to scrub all microbes from your food, but to proceed carefully and with a thoughtful eye on maintaining safety. By properly implementing the simple—yet powerful and effective—practices outlined here, the home fermenter should have no issues with harnessing helpful microbes and keeping harmful ones in check.

ABOUT THE BOOK

I have tried to organize the chapters in this book by specific fermentation types so that the types of fermentation build on one another. We begin with breadmaking, first with basic straight dough using commercial yeast (*Saccharomyces cerevisiae*) in chapter 2, then introduce bacteria, such as lactobacilli, and wild yeast with sourdough bread in chapter 3, before moving fully into the realm of lactic-acid bacteria with fermented vegetables, that is, pickles, relishes, and hot sauces in chapters 4 and 5. After that, we will dive into some simple cheesemaking and other dairy fermentations in chapter 6—more processes that lean heavily on lactobacilli—followed by a simple acetobacter fermentation in vinegar (chapter 7), then a more complex one in kombucha (chapter 8). The last fermentation we will discuss is meat, initially laying a foundation for fresh sausage-making and dry-curing whole muscles, then using those skills to ferment semicured sausages using lactic acid bacteria (chapter 9).

The recipes in this book will be a mix of wild fermentations that rely on whatever microbes are available on the food, or cultured fermentations that use an existing microbial culture. All of these existing cultures, which are nowadays available in pure, dried form, were used for thousands of years in a haphazard fashion. They were originally found by pure chance. Over time, people learned to create an environment hospitable to the desirable microbes and less welcoming of pathogenic bacteria. Eventually, people learned that there was something magical in a previous successful batch that could be added to the next batch to improve the chances of success, a method called *backslopping*. Now, we can isolate and grow pure biological cultures for our fermentations.

When making fermented foods, I rely on general cleanliness to prevent the introduction of a massive infection or contamination with unwanted biological material, but I do not generally worry about sanitizing equipment. Some people who ferment foods regularly, in particular those who do it for a living, will encourage you to use bleach or boiling water to minimize unwanted microbes. The fact is, we are surrounded by a tremendous variety of microbes at all times. This world belongs to microbes, and fermentation processes of all kinds were developed under decidedly non-sterile conditions (Katz 2012, 43). You will never ferment in a sterile environment, but if you create the right conditions for your indigenous or cultured microbes, they will crowd out any incidental microbes.

This mindset reinforces the sense of partnership that you, the one directing fermentation, have with the fermentative microbes you are trying to foster. Michael Pollan, when talking about people he knows who are into making their own fermented products, describes them as having "cultivated a relaxed and genuinely humble attitude to their work, which they regarded as a collaboration between species." He explained how "it helped to have the kind of temperament that could tolerate mystery, doubt and uncertainty without reaching for rule or reason" (Pollan 2013, 319).

The ingredients that you use also represent a partnership between yourself and those who work the land and create the ingredients you use: the farmer, the rancher, the butcher, the grocer. I hope that in your pursuit of fermentation, you will seek out fresh ingredients. This may be from a small grocer or local butcher that you trust, or a farmers' market, or even from growing your own. Whatever the case, pursuing fermentation with an eye on what is freshest will inevitably lead to you consider the question, "What is seasonal?"

These food preservation strategies evolved as a way to preserve seasonal bounty. We now live in a world where we can go to the grocery store in the middle of winter and find, say, asparagus, albeit thin and wilty. That might make an OK pickle, but it will not make a great pickle. It will not justify my efforts to preserve a mediocre, out-of-season ingredient. We may be able to buy anything at any time, and sometimes I am guilty of this, but I hope that learning some of these methods helps you to think more locally and more seasonally.

Thinking locally and seasonally means that what you have at your market may not match the things that I have at my local farm stand. However, I have tried to provide enough information that you can take some of these

Water Quality

Water quality, when water is called for in a fermentation, is of such paramount concern that it will be noted again and again. First and foremost, the water you use should look and taste good. It should not be brownish or cloudy, nor taste metallic or smell sulfurous (eggy), nor be excessively hard (which causes scaling). Some minerality is acceptable; calcium will actually aid in some of the processes laid out in this book.

City water is often chlorinated to fight microbial growth in water pipes. If you are unsure of the chlorine content of your water, carbon filter it or use another source, such as spring water or distilled water. Boiling water will drive off chlorine, though you will have to let it sit and cool afterwards. Bear in mind that boiling drives off chlorine but will not remove any chloramines. Homebrewers will be familiar with the use of Campden tablets, which are potassium or sodium metabisulfite. One Campden tablet will break down both chlorine and chloramines in up to 20 gallons (76 L) of water.

techniques and, with a little trial and error, figure out how to adapt regional ingredients to bring about your vision. My goal is to impart methods that can be adapted and applied to a variety of situations. There are recipes in this book, but it is not a staid, inflexible collection of recipes.

My overarching goal is to communicate the underlying requirements for making a good loaf of bread, pickle, or piece of charcuterie, and to explain what the levers are that you can pull to adapt the process to your needs and make something entirely your own. Michael Pollan explains this through the concept of "hand taste" in the Korean tradition, "the infinitely more complex experience of a food that bears the unmistakable signature of the individual who made it—the care and thought and idiosyncrasy that that person has put into the work of preparing it" (Pollan 2013, 416).

There are a number of books listed in the bibliography at the end of this book, but one of the best resources you can tap into is someone who has dedicated their career to the project you want to tackle. Offer to buy them a beer, ask if you can come in to help clean up one day, and they might let you pick their brain a little. At one time, before I began raising and butchering my own pigs, I was friends with a butcher at Whole Foods who was familiar with charcuterie and knew exactly what I was looking for when I told him what I wanted to make. He sometimes knew what I needed even when I did not. Cultivate those relationships. Maybe there is a home fermentation club or organization where you live. At a time when

you can buy a SCOBY from your favorite world-dominating e-commerce site and have it delivered the next day, maybe instead you could shop for one from a local kombucha-maker on Craigslist. They will probably be happy to share some tips and tricks too.

Weight versus Volume Measures

Almost all of the recipes and approaches in this book call for measuring key ingredients by weight. (There are things like spices or herbs that can be added with less precision, they may be noted in grams or teaspoons/tablespoons.) This is a crucial point. Different salts have different volumes. A packed cup of flour is significantly more than a sifted cup of flour. The way to develop a recipe that is replicable, or the way to make educated adjustments to a recipe that you are developing, is to be precise. The way to be precise is to weigh your ingredients and keep precise notes.

ABOUT THE RECIPES

My recipes here will generally reflect a preference for strong, bold flavors. Fermented foods tend to be the life of the party, adding punch to less exciting components, or sharpening rich foods with a hit of acidity. Redzepi and Zilber comment, "Once you have your first ferments, it makes cooking so much easier. . . . Once you integrate these ingredients into your cooking, your eating life is going to be irreversibly better" (2018, 14).

Everyone's preferences are different, and ingredients will vary from one location to another. My recipe for cured salmon that uses

"

Like a gardener, the brewer and the baker, the pickler and the cheese maker

all find themselves engaging in a lively conversation with nature.

All work with living creatures that come to the table with their own interests,

interests that must be understood and respected if we are to succeed.

— Michael Pollan,
Cooked: A Natural History of Transformation, p. 413

garlic, dill, and pepper can be much simplified for those who want the purity of the main ingredient to shine through, especially if they are working with salmon straight from the dock. (I can get good seafood in Colorado, but it will never be the same.)

One thing that experienced brewers and homebrewers should not need to be reminded of: write everything down. The secret to many of these methods is practice, careful observation, and good note-taking. Just as a good cook can turn a mediocre recipe into something delicious and a bad cook can render inedible a recipe from a Michelin-starred restaurant, the recipes contained in this book are only guides. Years ago, I disappointed someone who wanted my recipe "expertise" in helping him open a brewery. I explained to him that good recipes are a dime a dozen; what makes an excellent beer are excellent practices, and that is as true for food as it is for beer. Taking meticulous notes on weights, times, temperatures, and other variables will allow you to accurately refine your recipes and techniques from batch to batch. But in the end, just as with brewing, it must be remembered that these are living processes. There will be surprises, both good and bad. It is a partnership with the unseen.

FERMENTING WITH BEER

As wonderful as beer is to drink, it can also be a fantastic food ingredient. It can add citrusy, piney, fruity, and resinous hop notes, or malt flavors of breadiness, toast, caramel, chocolate, and roast. Sour beers can also include acidity and funky barnyard characteristics.

With all due respect to wine, there is not a beverage in the world that is as varied and diverse as beer.

In many cases, beer can be substituted for water in bread recipes. It can be used as a flavor ingredient in sausage-making and can be the base for vinegar. For bread and sausage-making, amber and darker beers (e.g., porter, stout, or brown ale) tend to work best—the lighter flavors of a Pilsner, pale ale, or even a tart Gose will be lost in the flavor of the final product.

Because of the factors that make beer relatively stable, using it in fermentations can be complicated. Hops are well known to have antimicrobial properties, as does alcohol. Either or both of these can inhibit or prevent the microbial activity necessary to produce a fermented food. Use high-ABV or hoppy beers cautiously and be open to some experimentation to find the right option. More than a few IBUs (international bittering units) from hops, even what you will find in a nice craft Pilsner, will slow or stop the activity of your lactic-acid bacteria, though these bacteria tend to be alcohol tolerant.

Flavor stability in beer can also be a factor. In vinegar, where the beer will remain as a liquid medium, more malt-forward beers may begin to show oxidized malt character. This may be a positive note, reinforcing some of the character in a barrel-aged beer, or it may create a stale, papery-tasting product.

I have included a few beer-based recipes in this work, such as a sausage made with German dunkel and a bourbon barrel–aged Baltic porter vinegar. They are great places to start, but by no means are they the last word.

2

BREAD

The value of bread in human history cannot be overstated. Grain, the seeds of certain grasses, was first ground between two stones some 15,000 to 30,000 years ago, and probably cooked as an unleavened flatbread. The next major advance in equipment came nearly 9,000 years ago with sieving, which helped to refine flour. In between, einkorn, a wild wheat, was domesticated 10,000 years ago, and about 8,000 years ago the first varieties of what a modern baker would still recognize as bread wheat were developed. The later development of stone mills and their modernization allowed further refining of flour.

Regardless of whether brewing or breadmaking came first as a driver of the transition from hunter-gatherer to domestication and agricultural life, "the emergence of grain agriculture gave rise to the earliest empires. The stability and storability of dry grains made possible unprecedented potential for accumulating wealth and building political power" (Katz 2012, 211).

However, grass species use that same storability to ensure the seed has the necessary nutrients for when it germinates. One way seeds store phosphorous—a vital nutrient—is within a compound called phytic acid. Unfortunately, the structure of phytic acid makes it very good at binding up dietary mineral content, earning it the "antinutrient" moniker. Phytic acid is concentrated in the cereal germ (the seed embryo) and bran, the hard layer of a cereal grain that surrounds the inner starch-laden part. While the germ and bran contain many valuable nutrients, the phytic acid also makes it difficult to absorb dietary minerals when digesting unrefined grain. Fermentation gets around this problem because it encourages the enzymatic breakdown of much of the phytic acid.

Similarly, cassava root, a key food for many tropical communities around the world, must be fermented to remove a naturally occurring cyanide precursor. While they may not have initially understood the chemistry behind it, indigenous peoples of the Americas discovered nixtamalization to treat maize (meaning the grain is soaked in water made alkaline with lime) to make it digestible, making maize a staple of the diet of those peoples. As Sandor Katz (2012, 212) noted, "Our ancestors intuitively understood or observed that grains and cassava roots need to be soaked (*which initiates microbial activity*) in order to be nutritious and easily digested" (emphasis added).

The transition from unleavened flatbreads to yeast-leavened bread, which happened at least 3,000 years ago, must have been a watershed moment in society. A risen loaf of bread that comes from a bowl of mush is "something that is much more than, and qualitatively different from, the sum of its simple parts" (Pollan 2013, 210). It is the alchemy of fermentation distilled down to its most dramatic.

Throughout modern history, the role of bread in daily life shaped culture and social norms. At times it was controlled by feudal lords who provided serfs their daily bread, which was the primary source of sustenance; at other times the type of bread you were allowed was determined by social codes or status.

In the West, wheat is the most common grain for breads and doughs, though corn, rice, and other grains are used in many other parts of the world. There is no crop grown today that is more important to humans than wheat. By acreage,[1] wheat is the largest food crop in the world, "waving its golden seed heads over more than 550 million acres worldwide; there is no month of the year when wheat is not being harvested somewhere in the world" (Pollan 2013, 226). Bread wheat makes up about 90% of the wheat grown; the remaining 10% is mostly durum wheat. The primacy of wheat has a long history. The original *Reinheitsgebot*, the German Purity Law limiting the ingredients allowed in beer, prescribed barley for brewing in Germany, since wheat and rye were needed to provide bread for the Teutonic masses. The baker's dozen,

meanwhile, originated in medieval England, when bakers would be under constant suspicion of selling underweight bread. Because of this, they would provide an extra loaf for every dozen sold to make sure they were never underselling.

The advent of the roller mill in the nineteenth century allowed for the creation of white flour, fundamentally changing how bread was made. Stone-milled flour could be sifted, but not fully separated. The roller mill, on the other hand, allowed for the three primary components of the wheat kernel to be separated: bran, the outer hull that makes up about 15% of the weight; the germ, which is a few percent of the weight and is composed of proteins, sugars, and lipids; and the endosperm, the energy store for plant growth, which is the bulk of the seed and is composed primarily of starch in a beta-glucan protein matrix.

In modern milling these three components of the wheat kernel are separated and mixed back together to create different types of flour, the most common being white flour versus wheat, or whole wheat, flour. The more bran and germ retained, the darker, denser, more nutritious, and more strongly flavored the bread will be. However, modern commercial bread, the bread created by the industrial revolution, is virtually pure endosperm.

Sadly, what passed as bread a hundred years ago is not what commonly passes for bread in the twenty-first century. Though wheat covers more acreage than any other crop in the world, the industrial bread that we have developed is a far cry from the agricultural product that sustained humankind for thousands of years: "There eventually came a moment when, propelled by the logic of human desire and technological progress, we began to overprocess certain foods in such a way as to actually render them detrimental to our health and well-being" (Pollan 2013, 254). While about 20% of the calories in the modern American diet come from wheat, almost all of it comes from white flour, which is about 70% starch, which, in turn, is nothing more than long chains of glucose molecules. In terms of dietary value, white flour is just a step above eating sugar.

Twenty-five to 30 percent of the seed that the American milling process discards is the

---

[1] Corn exceeds wheat by weight, but a large proportion of corn is diverted to animal feed or distilled for fuel.

most valuable: rich in vitamins, antioxidants, minerals, and healthy oils. That fraction often goes to feed animals, or to the pharmaceutical industry, the latter often recovering and repackaging those discarded vitamins to sell back to us as a supplement for our monotrophic diet of white flour (Pollan 2013, 253). In the 1940s, the commercial bread industry began fortifying bread with B vitamins to bring back part of the nutritional value that it had previously removed.

Harold McGee further laments modern bread's replacement of biological dough development, "the gradual, hours-long leavening and gluten strengthening of the dough by yeast, with nearly instantaneous, mechanical and chemical dough development" (2004, 520). These breads, with their soft interiors and "uncrusty crusts" are, instead, optimized for production speed and shelf life rather than flavor. They bear little resemblance to traditional breads.

Fortunately, there are bakers and authors out there who are working to create real bread that relies on craft and tradition—the return of a dark, crusty loaf (McGee 2004, 520). I want a crisp crust and tender crumb, subtle fermentation flavor, and a well-risen loaf to be our goals. Here, we will start with basic breads that consist of the four primary ingredients: flour, water, salt, and yeast. We will then augment those ingredients to introduce more flavor. Finally, in the next chapter, I will give you an introduction to sourdough baking.

FLOUR

Flour is the fundamental ingredient of bread. For our purposes, "flour" with no modifier (e.g., rye flour, garbanzo flour, spelt flour) refers to wheat flour. There are a variety of other materials that can be ground to flour, but wheat is our cornerstone. Most wheat varieties used for bread are the grass species *Triticum aestivum*, or common wheat. Wheat is the foundation for much of the Western baking canon because of its unique composition, including the presence of gluten-forming proteins.

About 10% of wheat is protein, and most (about 80%) of that protein consists of gluten-forming gliadins and glutenins. (The remaining

20% of wheat protein is mostly soluble protein that will contribute to the texture when baked.) Glutenin and gliadin combine to form the long gluten proteins that bond and create an elastic network in the dough.

Gluten gets a bad rap these days, but the gluten network created in dough allows bread to develop its desirable crumb structure. High-protein bread flour, followed by all-purpose flour, makes superior bread, while low-protein pastry flour produces a more crumbly, cakey consistency. Generally, all-purpose and bread flour rely on hard red wheat, which is higher in protein than soft white or red wheat. The bran flavor in white wheat also has a milder flavor than red wheat, which contains phenolic compounds that lend a more robust flavor to whole wheat flour ground from red wheat. Durum wheat is another option that can add a robust flavor to your breads. Look for finely-ground durum flour, if you decide to work with it.

Rye (*Secale cereale*) contains more sugars, more enzymes, more minerals and fiber, and ferments faster than wheat flour. It also contains pentosans, which are polymers built from five-carbon sugar molecules, that can create a gummy texture if overworked.

While whole-grain flour, both wheat and rye, is more nutritious, it also contains omega-3 fats that are present in the germ. These fats can oxidize after milling and go rancid within a few weeks. This has made white flour or sifted flour desirable for thousands of years as a more shelf-stable ingredient. As a result, the more nutritious and more flavorful whole wheat flour should be used quickly and stored cold if possible.

A good way to ensure that your whole-grain flour is fresh is to look for a local mill. A local miller knows the provenance of their grain and grinds flour only to meet near-term demand. Fresh flour will have more flavor, be free of chemical additives, and buying it supports local farmers, whose small businesses have been under siege by commodity agriculture for decades. You also might be able to find artisanal products like sifted whole wheat flour (which removes some, but not all, of the germ and bran), or unique blends of different wheats. My local miller, Dry Storage in Boulder, Colorado, offers flours ground from different heirloom wheats and blends of different flours for different purposes, including an all-purpose flour with enough germ and bran to lend extra character but not so much that it affects your recipe.

If you have to buy flour from the grocery store (and I do it sometimes, without hesitation), look for unbleached bread or all-purpose flours. In addition to avoiding unnecessary processing and chemicals, you will be getting a slightly more flavorful flour. Commercial millers in the United States often use azodicarbonamide or peroxide to artificially whiten the flour, which strips flavor as it removes the carotenoid that gives fresh flour a yellowish tint. (Over time, the carotenoid will oxidize to a paler color anyway.)

YEAST

During dough fermentation, the yeast interacts with the flour, digesting trace amounts of sugar and creating tiny air bubbles within the gluten matrix. While certain forms of quick baking make use of baking soda or baking powder for leavening, the fermented breads described here rely on yeast fermentation to create carbon dioxide in the starch-protein mass. (Self-rising flour contains baking powder; avoid it for general breadmaking.)

As bread dough rises, the yeast creates a network of carbon dioxide bubbles.

Wheat flour and rye flour contains amylases, which are familiar to brewers. These enzymes produce food for the yeast by breaking down starches into sugars. (Some commercial bakers add enzymes to their dough to increase this activity.)

The fermentation process will also be familiar to homebrewers and craft brewers: baker's yeast—*Saccharomyces cerevisiae*—consumes simple sugars and excretes a roughly 50/50 mix of ethanol and carbon dioxide (CO_2), as well as a variety of other trace materials. Instead of producing carbonation, the CO_2 bubbles produced in bread fermentation are trapped by the gluten network. During baking, the air pockets expand to account for up to 80% of the volume of a loaf, making the bread light and tender. (Both ethanol and CO_2 are volatilized in baking and driven out of the bread.)

As with beer, bread fermentation will proceed much more quickly at warmer temperatures, but fermentation closer to room temperature will give a slower rise and better flavor. As brewers know, a hotter, faster fermentation can create other unpleasant flavors compared to low and slow. Using less yeast also encourages flavor development at the expense of time, partly through the formation of esters and alcohols as the yeast multiplies, and also by allowing wild yeast and bacterial populations to multiply and add their own flavors. It is not an open-ended equation, though. Too long and the dough can overproof and collapse, or the flavor of the bread can become overly acidic.

Some bakers and authors favor an overnight proofing in the fridge—10 or more hours cold versus about one hour warm. Because proofing in the fridge is slow and cold (much of the activity occurs while the dough is going through its initial cool-down), the window where the dough is at an optimal condition before becoming overproofed is much wider, allowing for greater flexibility as you schedule your breadmaking. Rather than requiring a large portion of one day, the process can be broken up over a couple of days if it is convenient.

Others bread writers, such as Jeff Hertzberg and Zoe Francois (authors of *The New Artisan Bread in Five Minutes a Day*), are advocates of a similar method whereby the home baker mixes a large batch of dough and allows it, after an initial fermentation at room temperature, to continue fermenting and evolving in the fridge over days and even weeks. This technique relies on a very wet dough and develops a sourdough tanginess as it rests in the fridge.

Recipes in this book generally use active dry yeast at a rate of 1% of the grain weight. Instant yeast and cake (fresh) yeast are also viable options for bread baking; start with a 1:1 substitution of instant yeast or twice as much fresh yeast to replace the active dry yeast, and be ready to make some adjustments to your proofing schedule or your yeast amount as you get your recipe calibrated.

OTHER INGREDIENTS

There is a whole world of other potential ingredients that can be used in bread. These can add flavor, alter the texture, and change the color of bread.

Fats—butter, oils, lard—are called *shortening* because they literally shorten the gluten strands, weakening the dough structure. They create a softer, more tender, moister bread. Milk adds a little bit of fat and unfermentable sugar, providing a touch of richness and creaminess. The fat in eggs reduces gluten formation, but the proteins in eggs supplement the gluten structure with their own rise as they cook and coagulate.

A touch of sugar might be added to increase caramelization of the crust, but too much sugar will take up moisture that the gluten-forming proteins need, slowing gluten development in the bread. Malt extract or syrup is often called for in certain traditional recipes, such as pretzels. It primarily adds sugar to help browning, along with a touch of flavor.

Making cheese? Whey is a great source of moisture to substitute for water. It adds a bright, mildly acidic, additional note of fermentation to the bread. It is a good way to make use of everything, but do not expect it to have a radical flavor impact on your bread. All kinds of other liquids can add flavor to a dough: beer, wine, kombucha, I have even seen a recipe for bread made with pickle juice. If used at high levels, acidic ingredients such as beer, wine, or whey will affect the charge of gluten-forming proteins and can weaken the gluten structure of your bread.

To get a noticeable flavor note or recognizable acidity in the bread, you need a good bit of flavor or sourness in the liquid you use. I have used several varieties of lighter craft beers—Pilsner, pale ale, Kölsch, Gose—to minimal effect. Saison seemed like it would add complexity to a baguette, but the result was . . . subtle. Go for porters, stouts, or red wine. To double down on the flavor impact, you could even start with one-and-a-half to two times the necessary liquid; for example, if you need one 12-ounce (355 mL) bottle of porter, maybe pour one and a half bottles into a pot (drink the last half) and cook it down to the required volume, concentrating the malt and hop character that goes into the dough.

A wide variety of additional ingredients, such as herbs, spices, shredded cheese, chopped peppers, seeds, and many others can be added to your dough. However, breads with adjunct ingredients (herbs, spices, cheese, etc.) may not benefit from an extended fermentation or preferment, because these additional ingredients can overwhelm the subtle flavor differences in the fermentation flavor.

COMBINING YOUR INGREDIENTS

Turning grain into a risen loaf of bread involves a number of choices. What flours will you use, and at what proportions? How much salt will you use? How hydrated will your dough be? How much yeast will you use? How long will it ferment, and at what temperature? There are enough variables to make a whole world of breads with only flour, water, salt, and yeast. Michael Pollan likens the interplay of these variables to "a deft orchestration" (2013, 287).

The increasing availability of research and information is advancing home breadmaking at a dramatic pace. In the last ten to fifteen years, the use of a Dutch oven has gone from a cutting-edge innovation to a standard practice advocated in numerous excellent bread books. For decades, wet doughs had been a staple method in certain esoteric corners of baking but are now much more commonplace as the techniques have been disseminated more widely. The original publication of Jim Lahey's no-knead bread technique in 2006 was a watershed moment. These days, bread is being made more widely at home and professionally with more water, less yeast, less kneading, and more time for the natural process to take shape.

In baking bread, there are four primary stages or activities that have to occur: mixing ingredients, kneading or otherwise developing gluten, rising, and baking. These generally, but not absolutely, happen in that order. When using an autolyze rest (more on this later), you are helping gluten develop before adding all of the ingredients. Later, when letting a thin dough rise, you might fold it intermittently to develop gluten.

Our general method here will be to mix flour and water for an autolyze rest. An autolyze rest allows the flour to fully hydrate, which stimulates enzymatic action to spur gluten production. Then add salt and yeast, mixing well; fold as necessary early during the proofing; cut and shape prior to baking; bake; and, an easy-to-overlook final step, let rest.

When weighing out ingredients, I use separate containers for each ingredient. It is easy to overshoot and pour too much; it is much more difficult to remove excess water or flour once the two have been poured into the same vessel.

A small scale is helpful to measure out very small amounts of ingredients like salt and yeast.

Recipes here are based on the standard baker's percentage. The flour in the recipe equals 100 percent, and other ingredients are calculated from that. So, our baseline recipe of 500 grams of flour, 1% yeast, 2% salt, and 75% hydration means

$500 \times 1.00 = 500$ g flour,
$500 \times 0.01 = 5$ g yeast,
$500 \times 0.02 = 10$ g salt, and
$500 \times 0.75 = 375$ g water.

This is a good recipe size for testing recipes or baking for a small family; it will make three baguettes, one *batard* (torpedo-shaped loaf), or one small *boule* (a round loaf).[2] Boule recipes are scaled up to 750 g of flour to better fill a Dutch oven. These percentages are easy to double or even quadruple, if you like.

Understanding these percentages (and, yes, using the metric system) makes the math much, much simpler, allowing you to easily make adjustments, such as changing your hydration rate or substituting a percentage of whole wheat or rye flour into your dough. If you keep flour substitutions to less than 50% of your total flour weight (say, a 70/30 white/whole wheat blend instead of 100% white, or 20/15/65 whole wheat/rye/white flour), you should not have any trouble. Above 10%–20%, you will need to adjust the amount of flour down slightly, or the amount of water up slightly, to adjust for whole wheat flour's higher volume compared to the same weight of white flour, and its ability to absorb more water. King Arthur Flour (now King Arthur Baking Company) recommends a conversion rate of 113 g of whole wheat flour for 120 g of white flour.

A higher proportion of whole wheat or rye flour, or both, will affect how your bread rises. It can still be held to the same schedule, but it may be a little denser than if it had more white flour. If you decide to go above 50% rye and/or whole wheat flour, consider adding a tablespoon of vital wheat gluten per 250 g of whole wheat or rye flour. Because the additional germ and bran in whole wheat flour reduces the relative percentage of gluten-forming protein in whole wheat flour, breads with high percentages of whole wheat may not develop enough gluten structure to rise well, leaving you with an extra-healthy brick of bread. Vital wheat gluten is gluten that has been removed from wheat flour and turned into a powdered form. A small addition of vital wheat gluten can help your whole wheat flour loaf rise from a wholesome chore to a well-leavened delight.

The formation of gluten is essential to the fermented breads in this book. A lot of factors affect gluten formation, and it is possible to

---

[2]   *Batard* is French for "bastard," and is used to describe an oval shape in between the *boule* and the baguette. *Boule* is French for "ball."

adjust one variable to make up for another. As soon as water is added to wheat flour—and, to a lesser degree, to rye flour—the glutenin and gliadin proteins begin to combine and form gluten strands. However, it takes additional work to align and combine the initial random strands of gluten into a network that can elevate a loaf of bread.

The traditional method to develop gluten in bread is through kneading. Flour, water, salt, and yeast are all combined and the dough worked extensively to develop the gluten network. More kneading results in more even and smaller air pockets, while less kneading results in a more open, irregular structure. As the dough is kneaded initially, it will change in ways that are visually and tactilely obvious. It will gradually become a more cohesive mass, growing tighter and more difficult to knead. As it rests and rises, the gluten will relax and the dough might be folded a few times. Folding is where the baker stretches out the dough mass, folds one third on the side to the middle, then the third on the other side to the middle, then rotate the mass and do the same thing so you are folding new sections of dough. This helps to continue building the gluten matrix.

However, the French researcher Raymond Calvel determined in the 1970s that mixing the flour and water first without the salt or yeast allowed the flour granules to fully hydrate and helped the gluten-forming proteins to begin aligning without being kneaded. Increasing the level of hydration in the dough facilitates gluten formation as compared to a drier, stiffer dough. The impact of this additional moisture is so dramatic that it can replace kneading in the development of your dough. This is known as the autolyze method. The autolyze rest allows protease and amylase enzymes to begin to degrade the protein in the flour. Just like in brewing, these enzymes can work on your flour the same way it does in the mash. The proteases begin working on breaking down the proteins in the flour, while the amylases begin turning starches into fermentable sugars for the yeast so that you have a good rise. It also allows the flour to become fully hydrated and softened before it is worked. This is particularly valuable when using whole-grain flours, which contain knife-like shards of bran that

can tear up the gluten matrix and affect your rise. I use the autolyze method in virtually all of my breads at home, and it is an essential step in the recipes included here.

In practice, an autolyze step involves mixing your water and flour together until just barely incorporated into a ragged mass. Let this rest for 20 to 30 minutes, then add your salt and yeast. Gently mix the salt and yeast in and turn the dough out onto a floured work surface. Give it an initial fold, stretching it into a rectangle and folding the right third over the middle then the left third over the middle, then rotate the loaf or the board and repeat. Return the dough to its bowl and cover with plastic wrap or a towel. Periodically, the dough will undergo additional folds to further develop the gluten structure while it rises. The thinner (wetter) the dough, the more folds it will require. Another technique for folding, especially good with very wet doughs, is to reach to the bottom of the container holding your dough, grab the edge of the dough mass and pull it up the side of the container, folding it over the top of the dough. Rotate the container 90° and repeat this action until you have worked all the way around the container.

Loosely mixing the flour and water for an autolyze rest prior to adding the remaining ingredients allows the flour to hydrate and the gluten structure to begin forming.

Along with folding, the natural action of the rise (i.e., the development and expansion of CO_2 bubbles in the dough) provides some stretching and helps to develop the gluten structure. Salt is also critical for gluten development, not just flavor. Used at a rate of 1%–2% of the flour weight, salt improves the gluten

practice; you need to just keep an eye on the dough and learn, through practice, how to know when it is ready.

Really, truly great bread, like many of the foods in this book, is a product of both science and art. The recipes in this book will get you most of the way there. If you follow them and pay attention, you can make good bread. But the more bread you make, the more you will notice the intangibles—how long to mix your dough, when to stop shaping and let it relax, when it has reached that ideal level of proofing. When you do that, after many, many batches, you can begin to approach transcendent bread. But do not worry, you do not need to reach "transcendent" to make damn good bread.

Storing Bread

Bread, in particular loaves made from lean dough* using baker's yeast, has a narrow window where it is optimal.

During cooking, the starch goes from a crystalline to a gelatinized state, but as the bread cools and ages it reverts back to a crystalline structure, a process called *retrogradation*. Staling is the change in texture that accompanies this shift, as well as the bread losing moisture.

It may be counterintuitive, but refrigerating your bread actually accelerates this process. The starch reverts fastest at temperatures just above freezing, but very slowly below freezing. So, if you have made a big batch that will not get eaten promptly, the best way to store it is in the freezer.

Low levels of starch retrogradation can be reversed by heating the bread. Popping a slice of bread that is a few days old into the toaster helps it to quickly regain its former quality.

*A dough without added fat or sugar (or ingredients containing fat and sugar), usually consisting of only the four primary ingredients.

EQUIPMENT

Bread baking can be a relatively low-tech process, but a few handy tools make life much easier. Some kitchen basics like measuring spoons and measuring cups are always handy. A scale that measures in grams for weighing flour and water is essential, and a small scale that measures to tenths or hundredths of a gram is recommended to precisely measure tiny amounts of yeast. I like to use a plastic food-grade tub with volume markings to keep track of my rise, and plastic wrap or a kitchen towel to cover it. A bench scraper makes handling and cutting dough more manageable.

Proofing baskets are a helpful way to handle the wet boule doughs used in this book, and they impart a nice pattern on the dough that will impress friends and coworkers. (My chef friends like to remind me that we eat with our eyes first.) For baguettes and batards, a baker's *couche* or linen can be used to keep your shaped dough under control. A razor, paring knife, or baker's *lame* (blade) is necessary to score your dough.

For baking, a Dutch oven is extremely useful to get the best boule you can. A baking stone is important for batards and baguettes, and a baguette pan is also handy to help you maintain nicely shaped loaves. A steam water pan and a water spritzer will help you get steam into your oven for baguettes and batards. An oven thermometer can also help you make sure your oven temperature is properly calibrated. It is not uncommon for home ovens to run a little hot or a little cold. If you want to be baking at 460°F (240°C) but your oven is actually 430°F (220°C), it will affect how your bread bakes.

A kitchen timer is useful, if you do not have one on your phone. I have one on my phone, and one on my stove, plus two battery-powered kitchen timers, and on occasion have had all of them running during hectic holiday meals. A pizza peel is not just for pizzas; use it for anything you put on your baking stone.

Finally, once your bread is out, it needs to cool. A cooling rack is handy to allow air to circulate around your bread so the bottom does not steam as it cools. A serrated bread knife is essential to cutting your beautiful loaves.

Finally, a word of encouragement. Even though it is at the beginning of the book, breadmaking is one of the more challenging fermentations covered here. Do not be deterred by breads that did not come out the way you hoped. Your first few loaves, just like your first few homebrews, may not come out quite right. But when you finally put all the pieces together and pull a stunning loaf out of the oven, all the frustration will have been worth it.

Recipe Measurements

❭ Metric weights are used for baking recipes to give bakers the best results. A small, inexpensive kitchen scale can be purchased for this purpose and most new digital scales provide both metric and US weights and measures.

❭ US measurements for any added ingredients (e.g., cheese and nuts) are provided in parentheses.

❭ However, given this book was written with an American audience primarily in mind, oven temperatures and baking pan dimensions have been provided in US units first (metric in parentheses). Most American readers will be reaching for their favorite baking sheets sized in inches and setting temperatures on ovens that only work in Fahrenheit.

RECIPES

BAGUETTES/SANDWICH ROLLS

For years, this was my white whale. I love a good sandwich, and I always dreamed of making a baguette that was crusty on the outside with an open, airy texture. My loaves were decent, but always lacked that lighter-than-air crumb I was looking for. Sandwich rolls were good, but dense.

After more batches than I care to admit, I experimented with increasing my dough hydration, eventually hitting 75%. I could feel the difference in the dough as I rolled it out. As soon as that first batch came out of the oven and I hefted one of the loaves, I knew I had found the key.

A batch of baguettes scored and about to go into the oven (*left*), and right out of the oven (*right*).

Baguettes/Sandwich Rolls

Ingredients
- ○ 500 g all-purpose flour
- ○ 375 g unchlorinated water
- ○ 10 g salt
- ○ 5 g yeast

Directions
1. Mix flour and water into a shaggy mass in a bowl. Let rest for 20–30 minutes.
2. Sprinkle salt and yeast over the dough and knead for a few minutes until fully incorporated and the dough reaches a smooth, cohesive texture. Shape into a ball and place back into the bowl, covered with a kitchen towel or piece of plastic wrap.
3. Give the dough three folds spaced 20–30 minutes apart. Let it rise for a total time of 3 hours including the folds, or until the dough doubles from about one liter (1 qt.) to two liters (2 qt.) in volume.
4. After proofing, place a baking stone on a middle oven rack and a metal water pan (if using) on a lower rack and start preheating at 475°F (245°C) degrees. Cut the dough into three pieces (or six pieces for shorter sandwich rolls) and preshape on a floured work surface. Let the dough pieces rest for 15–20 minutes, then roll them out into their final shape and let rest an additional 40 minutes, uncovered. To create the proper crust for a baguette, the dough exterior needs to be allowed to dry prior to baking. At this stage, put shaped loaves into a baguette pan, if using.
5. One hour after preheating the oven and starting the preshape, score the loaves and put your baguette pan onto the hot stone or use a floured pizza peel to place the baguettes directly onto stone. Pour one cup (roughly 0.25 L) of water in your metal steam pan, if using; or add one cup of water to a glass pan, put the glass pan on a low oven rack, and give your bread a few sprays of water.
6. Cook for 12 minutes at 475°F (245°C), rotate your baguette pan or loaves 180 degrees, then cook another 12 minutes or until the top of the bread is nicely browned. Remove from the oven and let rest on a rack until the bread is cooled.
7. To make shorter sandwich rolls, cut the dough into six pieces instead of three. After shaping, put three into the fridge to slow the final rise. Once the first three rolls are baked, take the second set of three out of the fridge and allow the stove to reheat a few minutes before adding the second batch.

SOFT PRETZELS

Depending on how thin you roll them out, these can be thick, puffy pretzels, or thinner and larger pretzels. The bigger you make them, the harder they are to handle when flipping and taking them out of the baking soda solution.

Soft Pretzels

Ingredients

- 500 g all-purpose flour
- 360 g unchlorinated water
- 5 g yeast
- 12.5 g salt
- 7.5 g sugar
- 15 g barley malt syrup, malt powder, or honey
- baking soda (see step 5)

Directions

1. Mix flour and water into a shaggy mass. Let rest in a bowl for 20–30 minutes.
2. Sprinkle salt and yeast over the dough and knead for a few minutes until fully incorporated and the dough reaches a smooth, cohesive texture. Shape into a ball and place back into the bowl, covered with a kitchen towel or piece of plastic wrap.
3. Give the dough three folds spaced 20–30 minutes apart. Let it rise for a total time of 3 hours including the folds, or until the dough doubles from about one liter (1 qt.) to two liters (2 qt.) in volume.
4. Cut into 12 pieces and preshape into logs. Let rest 15–20 minutes, then roll out to about 22 to 26 inches long (55–66 cm), a little thicker than a pen. Shape into pretzels by forming the dough into a U, twisting the ends over each other twice, and folding the twisted end down to the bottom of the U. Press the dough ends into the dough at the bottom of the U. Let the pretzels rise 20–30 minutes on a floured work surface.

To shape pretzels, form the dough into a U shape. Twist the ends over each other twice, then fold them down to the bottom of the U.

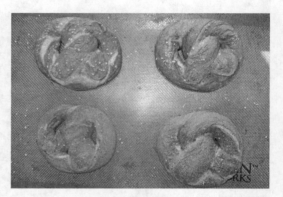

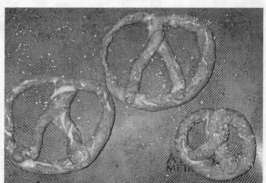

Depending on how thick you roll out the pretzel dough, you can make big, thin pretzels or smaller, bready pretzels.

5. Start preheating oven to 425°F (220°C). Put two to three inches (5–8 cm) of water into a large pot, adding one tablespoon of baking soda per cup of water (1 tbsp per 240 mL). Bring to a boil.

Soft Pretzels

© Getty/koldunova

Soft Pretzels

© Getty/koldunova

Soft Pretzels (cont.)

6. Working in batches, add pretzels into the boiling baking soda solution, as many as will fit without crowding. Simmer for 10–15 seconds, flip pretzels, simmer another 10–15 seconds, then move to a cooling rack to let drain. Do not worry if the pretzels plump up while in the baking soda solution and then look deflated.

7. Let pretzels drain and air-dry for a few minutes; before they are fully dried, sprinkle with coarse salt to taste.

8. Transfer pretzels to two or three well-oiled baking sheets, or baking sheets lined with nonstick silicone mats. Bake for 10 minutes at 425°F (220°C), rotate sheets 180 degrees, then bake another 5–10 minutes until nicely browned.

FOCACCIA

While pizza may be more common than focaccia in the United States, focaccia can be a truly decadent experience. A really good focaccia can be rich, and when topped with herbs, cheese, vegetables, whatever you like, can be paired with a salad for a delicious dinner.

This is a simple dough with plenty of olive oil to enrich the dough and help give it a nice brown crust. If you have access to 00 flour, this is the place to use it. An extra-refined flour developed in Italy, 00 flour contains similar levels of protein to all-purpose flour, but is ground more finely than other flours.

The combination of rosemary and parmesan makes an excellent topping for rich, hearty focaccia bread.

Focaccia

Ingredients
- ◯ 500 g all-purpose flour
- ◯ 200 g unchlorinated water
- ◯ 125 g whole milk
- ◯ 25 g olive oil, plus more for baking
- ◯ 10 g yeast
- ◯ 10 g salt

Directions
1. Mix flour, water, milk, and olive oil in a bowl until just incorporated. Let rest for 20–30 minutes.
2. Sprinkle yeast and salt over the top of the dough and mix until incorporated and dough is smooth and cohesive. Put in an oiled bowl and cover.
3. Let the dough rise for 2 hours, giving it three folds in the first hour. Or, after the first hour, store it in the fridge for up to a week.
4. After two hours, or when the dough has roughly doubled in size, preheat the oven to 425°F (220°C). Roughly shape the dough in an oiled 9" × 13" (20 × 30 cm) baking dish. If the dough becomes tight and does not want to stretch to fill the pan, give it 10–15 minutes to relax before coming back to continue shaping.
5. After the oven has been preheating for an hour, use your fingertips to dimple the dough, giving it the classically uneven look of focaccia. Drizzle olive oil lightly on the top

of the dough and along the edges, and sprinkle with salt. (If it seems like this is an excessive amount of oil, remember that focaccia is a rich, crusty bread. That is what makes it delicious.) Bake 25–35 minutes at 425°F (220°C). Remove from the oven and let rest on a rack until the focaccia is cooled.

Variations

Focaccia is a great canvas to add toppings to. A short, and by no means thorough, list of potential toppings includes herbs, olives, red peppers, onions, tomatoes (fresh or dried), garlic, nuts, prosciutto or pancetta, and cheese. Some of my favorite ways to top focaccia are rosemary and parmesan, or blue cheese and walnuts. But the sky is the limit, there is nothing precluding you from doing chopped bacon and jalapenos.

This dough is also good for pizza. I will sometimes split a batch of dough and make half of it as focaccia in an 8" × 8" (20 × 20 cm) baking dish, and roll out the other half of the dough a couple of days later for pizza.

Rosemary-parmesan focaccia: Prior to putting in oven, top dough with 60 g (2 oz.) shredded parmesan cheese and one and a half tablespoons of chopped rosemary.

Blue cheese-walnut focaccia: Before you start assembling the dough, take out a 225 g (8 oz.) chunk of blue cheese. Any soft blue cheese will do, but I like the sweet creaminess of gorgonzola dolce here. Let it come to room temperature while you are working on the bread. Once the cheese is warmed a little, put it in a bowl and add a splash of milk to make it a little more workable. Mix in 100 g (3.5 oz.) of chopped walnuts and spread this mixture over the top of your focaccia just before it goes into the oven.

Focaccia

PORTER BATARD WITH CHERRY AND FENNEL

Use your favorite porter here, something rich and chocolatey. Between the porter and the cherries, this bread is almost a dessert.

A porter with a rich malty or chocolate character really rounds out this delicious bread. Most of all, select a porter for this recipe based on what you enjoy drinking. © Getty/PavelKant

Porter Batard with Cherry and Fennel

Ingredients

- 500 g all-purpose flour
- 355 mL porter
  (equivalent to US 12 fl. oz.)
- 20 g unchlorinated water
- 5 g yeast
- 10 g salt
- 20 g fennel seeds
- 200 g dried cherries

Directions

1. Mix flour, beer, and water into a shaggy mass in a bowl. Let rest for 20–30 minutes.

2. Add yeast, salt, cherries, and fennel seeds. Knead for a few minutes until fully incorporated and the dough reaches a smooth, cohesive texture. Shape into a ball and place back into the bowl, covered with a kitchen towel or piece of plastic wrap.

3. Give the dough three folds spaced 20–30 minutes apart. Let it rise for a total time of 3 hours including the folds, or until the dough doubles from about one liter (1 qt.) to two liters (2 qt.) in volume.

4. After 3 hours, place a baking stone on a middle oven rack and a metal water pan (if using) on a lower rack and start preheating to 475°F (245°C). Preshape dough into an oval on a floured work surface. Let the dough rest for 15 minutes, then roll it out into a football-shaped oval and let rise an additional 40 minutes, covered.

5. One hour after preheating the oven, score the dough and use a floured peel to transfer the batard directly onto the stone. Pour one cup (roughly 0.25 L) of water in your metal steam pan, if using; or add one cup of water to a glass pan, put the glass pan on a low oven rack, and give your bread a few sprays of water.

6. Cook for 25 minutes at 475°F (245°C), rotate the dough 180 degrees using the peel, then cook another 15 to 20 minutes. Remove from the oven and let rest on a rack until bread is cooled.

FLATBREAD

Flatbreads are great for wrapping around grilled steak or lamb with some vegetables (grilled or fresh) and herbed olive oil. Or slice them up next to some vegetables to dip in hummus. Instead of the griddle, try cooking these on an oiled charcoal grill. It is a great way to spend the time while your grilled meat rests.

Flatbread
Ingredients
- ○ 500 g flour
- ○ 300 g unchlorinated water
- ○ 100 g yogurt
- ○ 10 g yeast
- ○ 10 g salt

Directions

1. Mix flour and water into a shaggy mass. Let rest in a bowl for 20–30 minutes.
2. Add yogurt, yeast, and salt to the dough. Knead for a few minutes until fully incorporated and the dough reaches a smooth, cohesive texture. Shape into a ball and place back into the bowl, covered with a kitchen towel or piece of plastic wrap.
3. Give the dough three folds spaced 20–30 minutes apart. Let it rise for a total time of 2 hours including the folds, until the dough doubles from about one liter (1 qt.) to two liters (2 qt.) in volume.
4. Divide the dough into six pieces. Preshape into balls and flatten out into circles. Let rest for 15 minutes or until the dough relaxes again, then continue stretching manually or using a rolling pin to roll out to ⅛" (3 mm) round pieces of dough. Do not stress if they are not perfectly round, there is nothing wrong with a more rustic look.
5. Preheat a flat griddle or cast-iron pan to medium heat. Cook, flipping a couple of times, until the flatbread is fully cooked and browned in spots.

Flatbread

Flatbreads make a great base for wraps, or can be used to mop up soups, stews, and sauces. © Getty/a_namenko

3

SOURDOUGH

We touched on the idea that longer fermentation times favor increased flavor development in the last chapter. In this chapter, we will focus entirely on building flavor through long fermentation and by harnessing wild microbes. There are no recipes for chocolate-raspberry-almond-stout loaves here, only ways to amplify the fermented deliciousness of bread.

However, the reader should consider this chapter as a postscript to the previous chapter on bread. The fundamental principles of bread baking that are laid out there are equally applicable to sourdough, so be sure to familiarize yourself with those concepts before diving in here.

The history of sourdough is, to an overwhelming degree, the millennia-long history of bread. Until the founding of microbiology and the isolation of yeast, less than 200 years ago, all bread was sourdough. From the first time that humans allowed their wheat gruel to age and get foamy before baking it into the first risen loaf, right up until the late nineteenth century when *Saccharomyces cerevisiae* was cultured and used in a pure form for baking, all bread relied on the natural presence of wild yeasts and bacteria.

The microbes in sourdough come from the air, from the baker's hands, the bowl and other tools, and most importantly, from the flour itself. Sourdough cultures contain a diverse array of microbial life, but the most common yeasts include *Candida humilis* (formerly *C. milleri*) and *Saccharomyces exiguus*. *Lactobacillus sanfranciscensis* was initially found to be present in the sourdoughs of California's Bay Area, home of the tangy San Francisco sourdough style, but has since been realized to be the dominant lactic-acid bacteria in sourdoughs around the world.[1]

These and other yeasts and bacteria create a microscopic ecosystem, with each strain filling a different role and eventually creating stability in the culture. As Michael Pollan explains, the baker is more of a guide than a commander:

It's a little like the difference between gardening and building. As with the plants or the soil in a garden, the gardener is working with living creatures that have their own interests and agency. He succeeds not by dictating to them, as a carpenter might to lumber, but by aligning his interests with theirs. . . .

This lack of control has never sat well with our species, which probably explains why the modern history of bread baking can be told as a series of steps aiming at taking the unruliness, uncertainty, and comparative slowness of biology out of the process. (Pollan 2013, 218)

In addition to sourdough breads, many cultures have a tradition of building flavor through preferments, fermenting part of the dough ahead of time with baker's yeast and then finishing the bread in a shorter period of time. These preferments can differ in thickness and percentage of the final dough—though even ostensibly the same method by name can also differ from one baker to another—but they include *biga*, *poolish*, sponge, and *pâte fermentée*.

Preferments rely on the idea of adding more flavorful, slowly fermented dough assembled a day or more ahead of time to fresh dough shortly before baking. In the previous chapter, we introduced the idea of overnight or mul-tiday fermentations of entire batches in the fridge to develop flavor and allow for flexibility in home breadmaking. Prefermentation relies on this same concept but cuts down how much of the batch is prepared ahead of time.

Preferments can use as little as a quarter of the final weight of flour and up to more than three-quarters. A large preferment that incor-porates most of the flour for a recipe provides the same benefits as an autolyze rest (p. 21). A preferment can be as thick as the final dough or can use a hydration rate of up to 100%. It can use the remains of a previous batch of dough. It can use small amounts of yeast and ferment for a long time at room temperature, or use more yeast with a longer fermentation at colder temperatures.

Time and temperature should be considered as ingredients just like yeast and flour. This approach does not treat the rise simply as a process necessary for gas to build up in the dough to give it structure, one that should take the shortest amount of time possible. Instead, you should view the rise as an opportunity to build flavor and an appropriate amount of acidity (Forkish 2012, 26).

Preferments can develop some of the same flavors as a sourdough culture; preferments from a sourdough culture are sometimes called a *levain*, where organic acids, esters, and alcohols from wild yeasts and bacteria add complexity. During baking, these compounds vaporize and are held in the bread's air pockets (known as alveoli) until they are released when the bread is eaten. The result is a multitude of volatile compounds (two hundred or so) reaching the back of the mouth and up into the nasal passages and are experienced by means of retronasal olfaction (Pollan 2013, 249).

Enzymes produced by the wheat, yeasts, and bacteria break down starches and proteins into sugars and amino acids to feed the microbes. In addition to helping feed the yeast, it makes the bread airier. As most brewers know, the chemical reactions between proteins and simple sugars in the presence of heat results in increased Maillard reactions, and heat also leads to caramelization reactions. For bread baking in the oven, these reactions produce the rich browning of the crust.

The increased acidity comes from bacterial growth, mostly lactobacilli, which is what gives the bread the sour flavor that is its name-sake. The acidity helps to activate the enzyme phytase, which breaks down phytic acid and makes minerals such as magnesium, iron, and

---

[1] You may find *Lactobacillus sanfranciscensis* is called *Fructilactobacillus sanfranciscensis* in more recent sources. They are the same microorganism. In light of new evidence, microbiologists reevaluate taxonomic classifications and species are sometimes moved to new genera. By the same process, you may find *Candida humilis* and *Saccharomyces exiguus* reclassified as *Kazachstania humilis* and *K. exigua*, respectively.

zinc that are bound up with the phytic acid become more readily available for your gut to absorb (see p. 15). The acidity of sourdough loaves allows them to age better and stale more slowly. Researchers have even found a strain in a French sourdough culture, *Lactobacillus hammesii*, that produces an antifungal agent. Breads containing some *L. hammesii* resisted mold for a few days longer than regular sourdough containing just *L. sanfranciscensis* and twice as long as bread made with baker's yeast.

Sourdough cultures also reduce the gluten content and some of the peptides that are thought to be partly responsible for gluten intolerance. The prevalence of modern breads with their very short fermentations have been thought partly responsible for the increase in gluten intolerance and celiac disease. What is more, the organic acids produced in a sourdough fermentation appear to slow the body's absorption of sugars from white flour, which reduces the occurrence of insulin spikes normally associated with eating refined carbohydrates (Pollan 2013, 229).

As Michael Pollan tells it, the process of making sourdough is also a very tactile, even sensuous process, forming a supple, delicate mass of gentle curves: "I have to say, not one of the bakers I had read or talked to had adequately prepared me for the erotics of leavened, shaped dough" (Pollan 2013, 232).

BUILDING YOUR SOURDOUGH STARTER

There are almost as many ways to get a sourdough starter going as there are users of sourdough starters, but let us dispense with some sourdough mythology right up front. Some people like to include fruit or juice, or whey, or a carefully curated selection of different flours. These different approaches may offer the comfort that comes with a sense of control, like a personal breadmaking ritual, but they are unlikely to change the final microbial culture you end up with. When you have non-flour food sources in your sourdough culture, you might initially encourage the growth of yeasts or bacteria that are specific to those food sources. But when you phase out those food sources, you are phasing out the yeast and bacteria

that specifically thrive on those ingredients. They are different microbes, evolved for different environments.

It is also romantic to think of using great-great-great-great grandma's sourdough starter that came with her from the Old World: "Legend has it that many immigrants brought their sourdoughs and other cultures dried on handkerchiefs" (Katz 2013, 231). But let us be real. Whatever yeast and bacteria are living on the flour you use to build or feed your sourdough starter is what will grow and thrive in your sourdough. Your yeast and bacteria selection is synonymous with your flour selection.

The best flour to start a sourdough culture is whole rye flour. Because it contains more available sugars and enzymatic content, whole rye flour will get your culture established a little faster than whole wheat flour. To start building a sourdough culture, mix a small volume of equal parts flour and water, 50–100 g of each. Wait two or three days and discard about three-quarters of the initial batch. Mix in new flour and water, and within a day or two you should see it begin to bubble and expand. At this point, you can transition to daily feedings, tossing all but 60 mL (a quarter cup, or 2 fl. oz.) of your sourdough culture prior to each feeding. I do not add salt to my sourdough culture until I am assembling my final dough, but salt does help to limit the protein digesting activity of lactobacilli, which can damage the gluten.

When you first start growing a sourdough culture, there will be a wide variety of microbes that are present. After the first few days of growth, though, lactic acid creates a hostile environment that kills off most of the early microbial colonists in your sourdough, leaving behind the hardier yeasts and bacteria that will create a vigorous ecosystem. In another week, these remaining microbes will find a balance that can be sustained with subsequent feedings. At that point, your sourdough culture is established and can be scaled up to use for bread.

I noted this in the previous bread chapter but is even more important when trying to propagate wild yeasts and bacteria: avoid chlorinated water.

USING YOUR SOURDOUGH CULTURE

Once you have your sourdough culture established, you can use your feedings and storage conditions to take it in a variety of directions. As Ken Forkish has learned in baking, "A true artisan baker is someone who understands how to manipulate the relatively small number of variables (which can yield an infinite number of possible results) to produce exactly the bread desired" (2012, 122).

In general, to feed your sourdough culture is to simply continue the feedings that you used to build the culture. Toss all but a teaspoon or two of the culture and add roughly equal parts flour and water (50–100 g) to what remains. Within these general parameters are a number of levers the baker can pull, depending on preference and convenience, to favor a more nuanced or a more robustly flavored sourdough.

Frequent feedings (daily or twice daily) and warmer temperatures favor yeast activity, while skipping meals and cool to cold temperatures favor bacteria, leading to a more acidic and strongly flavored bread. A warmer fermentation temperature favors lactic acid over acetic acid, while at colder temperatures the yeast is sluggish and vinegary acetic acid-producing bacteria become the dominant flavor-active agent. A denser feeding (say, 50%–60% hydration) slows down microbial activity, favoring yeast growth. A thicker culture traps more air, favoring the production of acetic acid (an aerobic metabolic pathway for bacteria) versus lactic acid (an anaerobic pathway).

You need to use whole-grain flour to feed your culture, because it contains more nutrients and a more diverse microbial population than white flour. There are 200 times more sourdough microbes in whole-grain flour versus white flour (Hamelman 2013, 423).

You can use a sourdough culture for 100% of the dough's leavening, or you can combine it with a pinch of commercial yeast to get the flavor of a sourdough with the lighter crumb of a bread made with baker's yeast. Whatever direction you decide to take your sourdough in, a vigorous starter culture is crucial, and your dedication to a healthy culture will be well-rewarded. If you are not going to use your sourdough culture for a while, it can be kept in the fridge. Pull it out once a week and let it warm up, then feed it right before it goes back into the fridge.

Sourdough is hardy. If you have missed some feedings and it is starting to smell pretty tart and funky in there, that does not mean it is time to start over. Just give the culture a few regular feedings and it will be right back to its baseline condition. From there, you can go back to pushing it in whatever direction you like. Your sourdough starter can also be safely frozen for months if you will not be using it often. A thicker culture, less than 70% hydration, will store better than a thinner culture. Freezing is stressful for the culture; some of the culture will have died, while some will survive and multiply when it is fed again. Frozen sourdough can be revived by feeding once it has thawed.

Prior to baking with your sourdough culture if you are storing it in the fridge, be sure to take it out a few days ahead and give it regular feedings. When you are ready to scale up your sourdough culture for a batch of bread, take a portion of your established culture, say 50 g (which would be 25 g of flour and 25 g of water), and add ten times that amount to it—in this example, that would be 250 g of water and 250 g of flour. Mix this starter together and let it ferment for four to six hours, until its volume has doubled. At that point, it is prime for use in a batch of bread. It may continue to expand past that moment, but if you wait too long and it begins to collapse, that means the fermentation is past its peak and will be less and less vigorous the longer you wait. The goal is to find that moment where the sourdough culture is propagated and at its most robust.

And finally, as with bread made with baker's yeast, it is important to practice, practice, practice. Sourdough is more difficult than straight dough, which itself requires a little understanding of timing, but stick to it.

"

It is definitely easier and faster to bake bread using a packet of yeast,

but it is a more magical experience to make bread by harnessing the power

of wild yeasts and bacteria, and the bread itself—in terms of flavor, crumb,

storage potential, and nutrient availability—is far superior.

— Michael Pollan, *Cooked: A Natural History of Transformation*, p. 237

Sourdough Scraps

It helps to keep your culture as small as is practical to avoid throwing away tons of discard at every feeding. Nonetheless, it can feel like a very wasteful process, especially if you scale up your sourdough, miss the window to bake, and have to rebuild your culture. Many home sourdough bakers have learned to use the discard for other baked goods such as rolls, waffles, pancakes, and biscuits.

In *The Art of Fermentation*, Katz recommends adding a little more flour/water (or not) and refermenting, some vegetables (or not) and an egg or two, some salt and cheese, and use the mix for a savory pancake batter.

Savory Sourdough-Scrap Pancakes

In addition to your sourdough scraps, this is a great vehicle for scrap meats, an extra pepper you might have sitting around, or even a spoonful of spring onion kimchi.

Savory pancakes are an excellent way to use up discards from feeding your sourdough culture.

Ingredients

- ○ 240 mL (1 cup) sourdough discard
- ○ 125 g (about 1 cup) flour
- ○ 1 egg
- ○ 2 teaspoons baking powder
- ○ 5 g salt
- ○ 240 mL (1 cup) milk
- ○ 50 g shredded cheese
- ○ A couple of slices of cooked bacon or some leftover sausage, diced
- ○ 2 scallions, trimmed and cut into ⅛" (3 mm) pieces

Directions

Mix all ingredients together in a bowl. Add another splash of milk if the batter is too thick. It should be thin enough to flow freely out of a measuring cup, but not so thin that it spreads to cover the entire surface of a pan.

Heat a skillet over medium heat. Add enough oil just to coat, then use a small (60 mL or ¼ cup) measuring cup to pour batter into the skillet. Cook 3-4 minutes until pancake is browned on one side, then flip. Remove when pancake is browned on both sides and cooked through. Repeat until batter is used up.

RECIPES

SPELT COUNTRY BREAD

Spelt, used here for 25% of the flour, is an ancient wheat hybrid with a more reddish color and a slightly nutty flavor that is sweeter and milder than regular whole wheat. Prefermentation is a great way to build layers of flavor with spelt, and when yeast is scarce this recipe is a great way to take a tiny bit of yeast and get the most out of it while also creating a bread with improved flavor. This recipe incorporates 75% of the total amount of flour into the preferment, adding just enough yeast in the final mix to give the last bit of flour a good rise. A *boule*, or "ball," is the classic round French hearth bread.

A sourdough boule incorporating spelt. Spelt flour is an excellent ancient grain to consider when looking beyond standard white and whole wheat flour.

Spelt Country Bread

For preferment
- ○ 375 g all-purpose flour
- ○ 188 g spelt flour
- ○ 450 g unchlorinated water
- ○ 2.8 g yeast
  (0.5% of baker's percentage)

1. Mix all preferment ingredients. Let ferment overnight, about 12 hours.

Final mix
- ○ 187 g all-purpose flour
- ○ 133 g unchlorinated water
- ○ 15 g salt
- ○ 3.75 g yeast (2% based on the final mix flour addition)

1. Combine final mix flour and final mix water; mix until just incorporated. Add final mix salt and yeast and the prefermented flour. Mix by hand to fully combine. Let rise 3–4 hours, until at least doubled in size. Fold three times in the first hour.

2. After the rise is finished, preshape into a ball and let rest, covered on a floured work surface, for 20 minutes. If the dough still feels slack, give it a final shaping.

3. Transfer to a floured bowl or proofing basket. Place a Dutch oven in the oven and preheat to 450°F (230°C). After an hour of preheating, gently invert the proofing basket over a floured work surface and turn the dough out. Score the dough.

4. Remove the Dutch oven and take the lid off. Very carefully put the dough into the hot Dutch oven, replace the lid, and put the Dutch oven back into the oven. Bake at 450°F (230°C) for 25 minutes, then remove the lid and bake for another 25 minutes or until nicely browned.

5. Once bread is baked, take out the Dutch oven and tilt it up to tip the finished loaf out, using a hand with an oven mitt or towel to catch it (the bread will still be very hot). Allow to cool on a rack for at least an hour before cutting.

Spelt Country Bread

SOURDOUGH BOULE

With a crusty exterior and airy, slightly tangy crumb, this sourdough boule is delicious fresh and stays good for several days. This recipe is scaled to fit a five-quart (~5 L) Dutch oven. It can be prepared and baked in a day, or fermented cold for up to a few days and then baked.

In addition to containing your dough, proofing baskets give sourdough loaves a distinctive, appealing pattern.

Sourdough Boule

For initial sourdough propagation
- 40 g healthy sourdough culture (I use a 100% hydration rate, or a 1:1 flour-to-water ratio.)
- 200 g unchlorinated water
- 200 g flour (You can use white flour here, but I generally use whole wheat flour, making this a 25% whole wheat loaf.)

1. Combine culture with flour and water. Let rise 4–6 hours, until at least doubled in size.

For final dough
- 375 g propagated sourdough culture, as close to fermentation peak as possible
- 563 g white flour
- 375 g unchlorinated water
- 15 g salt

1. Combine remaining flour and water in a separate container and mix to a shaggy mass. Because the sourdough culture is hydrated at 100%, this second portion of the dough will be much thicker. Let rest for 20 to 30 minutes to hydrate the flour.

2. Add salt and 375 g of sourdough culture to the autolyzed (rested) flour/water mix. (Give the remaining sourdough culture a feeding and store it for later use.) Mix until fully combined.

3. Fold three times during the first hour, then put into the fridge overnight. Or, for same-day cooking, let rise for 3 hours after folds are completed or until at least doubled in size. Preshape into a ball and let rest, covered on a floured work surface, for 20 minutes. If the dough still feels slack, give it a final shaping. Transfer to proofing basket. For cold-fermented dough, remove the dough from refrigeration about 90 minutes before baking. Preshape, rest, shape, and transfer to a proofing basket as described for same-day baking above.

4. Once dough is shaped, place a Dutch oven in the oven and preheat to 450°F (230°C). After an hour of preheating, gently invert the proofing basket over a floured work surface and turn the dough out. Score the dough.

5. Remove the Dutch oven and take the lid off. Very carefully put the dough into the hot Dutch oven, replace the lid, and put the Dutch oven back into the oven. Bake at 450°F (230°C) for 25 minutes, then remove the lid and bake for another 25 minutes or until nicely browned.

6. Once bread is baked, take out the Dutch oven and tilt it up to tip the finished loaf out, using a hand with an oven mitt or towel to catch it (the bread will still be very hot).

7. Allow to cool on a rack for at least an hour before cutting. The flavor of this bread will develop and improve over a couple of days.

WHOLE WHEAT SOURDOUGH

This is a robustly flavored sourdough that, between the sourdough culture and the second addition of flour, consists of 50% whole wheat (25% in the initial propagation and 25% in the final mix). A little vital wheat gluten helps leaven the loaf under all that whole grain. There is a ton of moisture-sucking protein in this recipe, though, so we bump the hydration rate from 75% up 80% to make it easier to handle. Like the recipe above, the flour here is 763 g, sized for a five-quart (~5 L) Dutch oven.

The boule, or ball, is a classic shape for hearth breads like sourdough.

Whole Wheat Sourdough

For initial sourdough propagation
- ○ 40 g healthy sourdough culture
- ○ 200 g water
- ○ 200 g whole wheat flour

1. Combine culture with flour and water. Let rise 4–6 hours, until at least doubled in size.

For final dough
- ○ 375 g sourdough culture
- ○ 375 g white flour
- ○ 188 g whole wheat flour
- ○ 413 g unchlorinated water
- ○ 15 g salt
- ○ 15 g vital wheat gluten (about 1½ tablespoons)

1. Combine remaining flour and water in a separate container, mix to a shaggy mass. Because the sourdough culture is hydrated at 100%, this second portion of the dough will be much thicker. Let rest for 20–30 minutes to hydrate flour.

2. Add 375 g of sourdough culture to autolyzed (rested) flour/water mix, then sprinkle salt and vital wheat gluten on top. Mix until fully combined.

3. Fold three times during the first hour, then put into the fridge overnight. Or, for same-day cooking, let rise for 3 hours after folds are completed or until at least doubled in size. Preshape into a ball and let rest, covered on a floured work surface, for 20 minutes. If the dough still feels slack, give it a final shaping. Transfer to proofing basket. For cold-fermented dough, remove the dough from refrigeration about 90 minutes before baking. Preshape, rest, shape, and transfer to a proofing basket as described for same-day baking above.

4. After dough is shaped, place a Dutch oven in the oven and preheat to 450°F (230°C). After an hour of preheating, gently invert the proofing basket over a floured work surface and turn the dough out. Score the dough.

5. Remove the Dutch oven and take the lid off. Very carefully put the dough into the hot Dutch oven, replace the lid, and put the Dutch oven back into the oven. Bake at 450°F (230°C) for 25 minutes, then remove the lid and bake for another 25 minutes or until nicely browned.

6. Once bread is baked, take out the Dutch oven and tilt it up to tip the finished loaf out, using a hand with an oven mitt or towel to catch it (the bread will still be very hot). Allow to cool on a rack for at least an hour before cutting. The flavor of this bread will develop and improve over a couple of days.

SEEDED SOURDOUGH BATARD

I like an even mix of rolled oats, sunflower seeds, and quinoa, but a wide variety of other seeds and nuts are good here. You will need to soak them for a few hours ahead of time, otherwise the seeds can pull moisture out of your dough and throw off the hydration rate.

A variety of seeds and grains can be used to infuse the bread with additional flavor, and provide visual impact and textural contrast.

Seeded Sourdough Batard

For initial sourdough propagation
- 40 g healthy sourdough culture (I use a 100% hydration rate, or a 1:1 flour-to-water ratio.)
- 200 g water
- 200 g white or whole wheat flour

For seed soaker
- 150 g seeds and nuts (a combination of rolled oats, sunflower seeds, quinoa, toasted pine nuts, fennel seeds, flax seeds, poppy seeds, sesame seeds, or whatever else may entice you)

1. Combine culture with flour and water. Let rise 4–6 hours, until at least doubled in size.
2. After sourdough propagation is started, mix seeds with 100 g water. Let soak until added to the final dough.

For final dough
- 375 g propagated sourdough culture, as close to fermentation peak as possible
- 563 g white flour
- 375 g unchlorinated water
- 15 g salt

1. Combine remaining flour and water in a separate container and mix to a shaggy mass. Because the sourdough culture is hydrated at 100%, this second portion of the dough will be much thicker. Let rest for 20–30 minutes to hydrate flour.
2. Add salt and 375 g of sourdough culture to autolyzed (rested) flour/water mix. (Give the remaining sourdough culture a feeding and store it for later use.) Drain off any excess water in the seeds and add seeds to the dough. Mix until fully combined.
3. Fold three times during the first hour, then put into the fridge overnight. Or, for same-day cooking, let rise for 3 hours after folds are completed or until at least doubled in size. Preshape into an oval and let rest, covered on a floured work surface, for 20 minutes. Shape dough into a batard (a short baguette) and cover. For cold-fermented dough, remove the dough from refrigeration about 90 minutes before baking. Preshape, rest, shape, and transfer to a proofing basket as described for same-day baking above.
4. After dough is shaped, place a baking stone on a middle oven rack and a metal water pan (if using) on a lower rack and start preheating at 475°F (245°C). After an hour of preheating, score the dough and use a floured pizza peel to transfer the batard directly onto the stone. Pour one cup (roughly 0.25 L) of water in your metal steam pan, if using, or add one cup of water to a glass pan, put the glass pan on a low oven rack, and give your bread a few sprays of water.
5. Cook for 25 minutes at 475°F (245°C), rotate the dough 180° using the peel, and cook another 15 to 20 minutes.
6. Allow to cool on a rack for at least an hour before cutting.

Sourdough Boule

4

PICKLES, SAUERKRAUT, KIMCHI

Fermented vegetables are a staple food around the world. As a way to preserve the harvest bounty, to add nutrients and punch to a peasant meal that may otherwise consist simply of porridge or rice, to convert the inedible into the delicious, or to just round out a modern grain bowl or cheese and charcuterie plate, pickled vegetables are irreplaceable. Today there are many reasons brewers are fermenting at home, not least flavor, wellness, and a connection to nature and simplicity. Fermentation is "one of the oldest and simplest means of preserving food" as it requires no cooking or special climate (McGee 2004, 291). In many cases, all that is necessary is salt and a container.

In *Japanese Cooking: A Simple Art*, Shizuo Tsuji's authoritative book on Japanese food, the importance of rice and pickles as staples is made clear: "Pickles are a vast domain in Japanese cuisine. There is a seemingly endless variety of both delicate and strong pickled foods, preserved in all sorts of ways, and they play an important role in the dietary life of the people" (Tsuji, 2011, 51). Korean kimchis encompass a wide variety of ingredients and methods, from quick-fermented summer kimchis, some of which are more like light summer soups than pickles, to hearty cabbage kimchis traditionally buried in stone crocks for months on end. Europeans learned to ferment cabbage from the Chinese or Mongols, leading to a tradition of sauerkraut (or any number of other names in local languages) in many European cultures.

Italy developed a tradition of making *giardiniera* to preserve whatever summer vegetables were bountiful, usually cauliflower, celery, carrots, and bell peppers. Latin America has a tradition of curtido, pickled vegetables, and *escabeche*, the last one originating as a method of cooking meat and preserving it in an acidic mixture, but which has since grown to include pickled vegetables in Mexico. In the United States, cucumbers are the vegetable most associated with the word "pickle," and they have a history of being preserved that goes back thousands of years to the Middle East and Asia.

Fermented vegetables are pickled, that is, preserved in acid, but are different from commonly found grocery store pickles that are packed in vinegar and pasteurized. They have a different flavor profile and are full of live cultures. All kinds of vegetables can be fermented. Great starting points include green beans, cauliflower, cucumbers, carrots, and okra.

Pickled okra is a delicious tradition in the American South.

Fermented pickles rely on bacteria for acidification, converting plant sugars into lactic acid, carbon dioxide (CO_2), trace amounts of alcohol, and other compounds. These halophilic (salt-tolerant) anaerobic bacteria are everywhere, as are unfriendly bacteria, viruses, and yeasts. When making fermented pickles, you use salt or brine to create a salty, oxygen-free environment, which is hospitable for the bacteria you want and hostile for the microbes you do not want. This will allow the desirable bacteria to outcompete the spoilage

microbes. Lactic-acid bacteria will lower the pH of the vegetables to a level that will prevent the growth of pathogenic bacteria. In addition to creating acidity that will keep other microbes at bay, the fermentation of vegetable sugars also removes a primary food source for competing bacteria and yeasts.

Leuconostoc mesenteroides is the dominant lactic-acid bacteria in the initial stages of vegetable fermentation. *Leuconostoc mesenteroides* will produce an elevated level of CO_2, purging any remaining oxygen from the fermentation environment to allow for strict (obligate) anaerobes. A facultative anaerobe, *Leuconostoc mesenteroides* will also take up the available oxygen and produce small amounts of acetic acid.

Once the pH of the vegetable fermentation drops too far for *Leuconostoc mesenteroides*, it goes dormant and *Lactobacillus plantarum* takes over. *Lactobacillus plantarum* produces lower levels of CO_2 so the fermentation may appear to stall based on the bubbling in your fermentation vessel, but you should judge doneness by taste.

The amount of sugar in the vegetables, which will feed the bacteria and allow them to create organic acids, will define the level of acidity in your finished pickle. A higher sugar content means more food and more microbial activity, and result in high levels of acids. *Lactobacillus plantarum* can remain active down to nearly pH 3.0, well below the point at which your pickle will finish fermenting without the addition of extra sugar. Pickling cucumbers, with about two percent fermentable sugars, are at an ideal spot—with complete fermentation the pH should drop into the low 3s. A pH of 4.6 (roughly the acidity of a fresh tomato) or below is recommended for fermented vegetables; below that, *Clostridium botulinum* growth is inhibited. While a vegetable fermentation will not immediately fall below pH 4.6, clostridial spores will be outcompeted and will not germinate as long as lactic-acid bacteria are multiplying and the pH is dropping.

It is not a necessity for pickling, but an easy handheld pH meter can be found for about US$50 for those who want to keep close tabs on their fermentations. If you do decide to track the pH of your ferments, be sure to get

Beware of microbial growth aside from Kahm yeast. Small bits of growth on floating pieces of vegetables, if caught quickly, can be skimmed off without ruining the fermented vegetable, but batches with significant growth should be discarded.

Kahm yeast can create a white film, sometimes capturing CO_2 bubbles, on top of a brine. It is not harmful, but can be skimmed off to prevent it from imparting a yeasty character to the food.

calibration solutions to make sure your meter is reading accurately. For fermented vegetables, though, I generally just look for the brine to become cloudy after a few days (that's the bacterial culture multiplying and getting to work), followed by CO_2 bubbling out. After a couple of weeks, or after being transferred to the refrigerator to slow the fermentation down, the bacteria will become less active. You will see sediment at the bottom of the jar and the brine will begin to clarify.

Fermenting vegetables in the traditional manner, submerged in brine or salted and pressed below the level of the moisture exuded from the vegetables, is fundamentally safe. Everything that stays submerged in brine will stay safe to eat. With some ferments, you will have pieces of vegetable that escape, floating to the surface and growing mold. Just skim them off.

The lactic acid and salt create a relatively, though not completely, stable environment. Kahm yeast is a common occurrence in fermented vegetables; it creates a thin white film that may capture large CO_2 bubbles. It can leave a slightly yeasty flavor in your pickles if it is allowed to thrive. Keep an eye on your ferments, even in the fridge, and remember that they are living things. Some of them can last a long time, but not forever. The bacteria and enzymes are continuing to act, continuing to break down your vegetables. Let your taste buds be your guide.

In *The Art of Fermentation*, Sandor Katz noted that "incidental" contamination by pathogenic microbes—the kind that has caused outbreaks in recent years of foodborne illnesses traced to raw vegetables like spinach and lettuce—would not occur in a proper fermentation environment:

I think it would be fair to say that fermented vegetables are safer than raw vegetables. For even given some freak incident of contamination, the incidental pathogenic bacteria could never compete with the native lactic acid bacteria populations, and the acidification that rapidly develops in fermenting vegetables would destroy any surviving pathogens. Lactic acid bacteria offer a strategy for safety and preservation that is present in all vegetation. (Katz 2012, 96)

Katz observes that there have been outbreaks of botulism from the preservation of garlic in olive oil, an ideal environment for *C. botulinum* (see p. 10). However, the acidity produced in fermentation creates an environment safe from *C. botulinum*.

It must be added that using vegetables of questionable quality to begin with can produce pickles of questionable safety if not fermented completely enough. If they are already present at hazardous levels, *E. coli*, listeria, and salmonella bacteria can survive through the initial stage of fermentation and pose health risks until the pH drops far enough. A 2012 outbreak of *E. coli* that affected more than 1,600 South Korean students was linked to radish and cabbage kimchis that may not have been processed safely or may have used contaminated ingredients.

Therefore, it is strongly recommended to only ferment vegetables you are already comfortable eating, and not rely on fermentation to make questionable vegetables safe. If the vegetables are safe before you ferment them, they will be safe after you ferment them. (And yes, you can wash your vegetables before fermentation without worry about removing the necessary fermentation bacteria. Just do not pour boiling water over them or soak them in sanitizer.)

While microbial acidification is the primary force in stabilizing pickled vegetables and keeping them safe, salt plays a significant role as well. The level of salt in your pickles is a crucial choice. It draws out moisture from the vegetables via osmosis, dehydrating them slightly. This creates a less hospitable environment for pathogenic bacteria, tilting the scales in favor of desirable bacteria, and it slows the enzymatic activity that softens vegetable matter. Too little salt and your food will be bland; too much and it will be inedible.

All other things being equal, a higher level of salt will give you crisper fermented vegetables. Because the fermentation process involves the bacterial cultures penetrating the vegetables to digest the available sugars, fermented pickles will not retain the same level of crispness as vinegar pickles. Since the rate of fermentation is inversely related to the size of the vegetable pieces (larger or thicker pieces will ferment more slowly), you can try to offset this a little bit by fermenting whole vegetables and refrigerate them before fermentation has fully penetrated the vegetable. It will still continue to soften in the fridge, but at a much slower rate. (However, it is possible, and done at the commercial level, to ferment and store pickles in a high-salt environment that maintains the integrity of the pickle for a year or longer. These pickles need to be purged of some salt prior to being eaten.)

Brines are calculated based on the weight of the water: for example, a 5% brine is one where salt is added at a rate of 5% of the water weight, so 1,000 g of water plus 50 g of salt in this case. I generally use a brine of 4%–6%, knowing that the salt concentration will be diluted by the vegetables. Salting for dry-brined ferments, where salt and spices are added to the vegetables without additional water, is based on the overall weight of ingredients and tends to be lower. These fermentations rely on the vegetables releasing moisture that creates a brine, so the vegetables will need to be weighed down to stay submerged.

Overall, fermented vegetables generally fall into the range 2%–5% salt by weight. Rene Redzepi reports that his restaurant, Noma, uses 2% salt based on the total weight of vegetable and water. A lower salt content will leave the fresh vegetable flavor more intact, but the lower you go, the less inhibitive action the salt will provide to help lactic-acid bacteria to dominate.

In addition to salt, I will often add a big, four-finger pinch of calcium chloride (an addition familiar to many experienced homebrewers) to help pickles stay crisp for the long term. According to Katz, commercial pickle producers may use calcium chloride to 0.1–0.4% (Katz 2012, 124). At the grocery store you can look for Pickle Crisp® to serve the same function. Grape, oak, or horseradish leaves, which are rich in tannins, can also be added to help retain crispness.

In general, a fermentation temperature in the 68–72°F range (20–22°C) is as comfortable for lactic-acid bacteria as it is for humans. Too hot, and the fermentation will proceed faster but can potentially create off-flavors. Too cold will slow fermentation down, potentially resulting in a sluggish or stalled fermentation. It is possible to ferment in the fridge, it will just take a long time. Because increased levels of salt will also slow fermentation, Katz advises using more salt to counteract the heat of summer and slow things down, and less salt in the winter to let fermentation proceed a little faster (Katz 2012, 100).

There are myriad ways to prepare vegetables for different fermentations. You can do whole vegetables, with or without seasonings or spices (e.g., green beans, pickled cucumbers), break down your vegetables into smaller pieces to ferment (think pickle slices/spears or sauerkraut), use a primary vegetable with other vegetables mixed in as seasoning (e.g., kimchi), or assemble a mixed fermentation (e.g., escabeche, giardiniera).

The smaller you break down the vegetables, the faster the brine will penetrate them, or the faster water will be exuded to form your brine. Shredded cabbage for sauerkraut will release moisture faster than the chopped or whole cabbage used for kimchi, and cucumber slices will take less time to be fully brined and fermented than whole pickles.

When packing vegetables into jars to ferment, it is important to leave a half inch or more (1–2 cm) of headspace, and a couple of inches (5 cm) in a crock, to keep a vigorous fermentation from bubbling over. Pickles will ferment and evolve over several days and weeks. I often start tasting from a large batch after CO_2 production slows. This is the point, when gas production drops off, that *Leuconostoc mesenteroides* becomes inactive and *Lactobacillus plantarum* becomes the primary active culture. Even after the initial few weeks, fermentation will continue to penetrate hard or large vegetables like carrots or whole cucumbers.

Your fermentation is done when you are happy with it. In some ferments, like summer kimchi, a day or so is enough. For escabeche, as with many pickled vegetables, there is an evolution as the vegetables ferment and acidify, going from salted, fresh vegetables to tart, softening pickles. For smaller vegetables, a week or two (or in the winter, maybe 10–20 days) is good. I will give jars on the counter an occasional jostle to see if they are still bubbling, and give the brine or pickles a taste. If you have a ferment with a mix of vegetables, the fermentation may finish but the flavor of the different ingredients will continue to merge and blend together. Just keep tasting and you will start to understand how the fermentation flavor evolves and where you like it best. You may prefer a partial ferment, traditionally called a half-sour pickle. You may enjoy your escabeche at different stages and decide to put half of if it into cold storage after two weeks while allowing the other half to continue fermenting at room temperature for another few weeks.

Check your jars periodically, giving them a burp every day or two to check the status of fermentation and prevent pressure from building up, especially in glass jars. It is also important to make sure everything remains submerged, otherwise vegetable matter that is sticking up above the brine level can start to mold. If that happens, you can remove those pieces and skim off the mold from the top of the ferment. If you have caught it quickly enough, the rest of the batch will still taste fine. Finally, do not expose your fermentations to direct sunlight (remember, UV light is a disinfectant), but indirect ambient light on the kitchen counter is fine.

Community Fermentation

Are you a gardener? A homebrewer? If so, odds are you know other people who are as well. Start a fermentation club, or organize friends who are interested in branching out into fermented foods. Fermented vegetables are a great place to start. Some vegetables grow so abundantly that they almost require sharing (or, alternately, you can eat squash and cucumbers every day for three months). Everyone can choose a vegetable to grow, ferment, and share with the group. Instead of five people making sauerkraut for themselves, everyone can share a different fermentation; each person might get kraut and/or kimchi, pickled cucumbers, pickled green beans, hot pepper sauce, and tomatillo salsa. Or your group can put together your own combination of vegetables for a giardiniera, where every member contributes a vegetable to a large batch that gets split among the group. It is a great way to build community, and the possibilities are endless.

EQUIPMENT

When making and storing pickles, be sure to use glass, plastic, stainless steel, or nonreactive ceramic containers. Over the years I have amassed a collection of stuff that ranges from as small as a few fluid ounces (60 mL) up to as big as a hotel pan or an 18-quart (~17 L) plastic food tub. I have some crocks that I use for "dry" salted ferments, like sauerkraut, and jars of varying sizes from three or four ounces (90–120 mL) of an intense hot sauce, up to gallon-size (3.8 L) jars for whole pickles. Half-pint (240 mL) jars are a great place to start when experimenting with new recipes. These little jars allow you to make one batch of brine, then split it and season your pickles differently (e.g., lemon/dill, garlic/jalapeno). Stone weights sized for ceramic crocks are generally available, and there are tempered glass stones sized

A variety of options are available to weigh down your fermenting vegetables. Sometimes a smaller jar is just the right fit for a larger jar.

A mandolin is a tremendously helpful tool for breaking down large amounts of vegetables, such as cucumbers, that will be made into pickle slices.

for both regular and wide-mouth canning jars to help keep your vegetables submerged. You can also cut a round piece of plastic cheese mat and follow it (known as a follower) with a zip-lock bag of brine to weigh your fermentation. A few sources note the age-old tradition of using a whole cabbage leaf as a follower, with a weight on top.

You may or may not need a final cover on your fermentation, depending on your equipment setup. Jars generally come with a lid, and a properly sized ziplock bag will fill the whole space and create a mostly airtight seal in whatever container you are using. If you just have a couple of stones and some brine exposed to the air, or you have a follower that does not give you a complete seal, you might want to put a cover or at least a piece of cheesecloth over the top to keep out flies and bugs, and possibly a layer of plastic wrap if your fermentation runs the risk of drying out.

If you are forgetful and might not stay on top of burping your jars, there is a variety of equipment available that will help, from airlock systems that allow CO_2 to escape, to extractors that pair with custom lids and are used to pull air out of the fermentation jar. Brewers have the advantage of having airlocks around and can easily drill a hole and add a traditional airlock. It works brilliantly and there is no need to "burp" the jars. A tamper is handy for pounding traditional cabbage ferments to break down the cabbage and release moisture faster. If you are processing a large volume of vegetables, a mandolin or cabbage shredder can quickly pay for itself in time saved. But be sure to buy a couple of cut-resistant gloves. The razor-sharp slicer of a mandolin is awesome for making ridged pickle chips, but if you are not extra careful it will take a ridged piece of your finger off as well.

RECIPES

MAKING A BRINE

Most of the recipes in this chapter use a brine to cover the vegetables. The strength of the brine is usually 5% but this may differ for certain recipes. When making your brine solution, the metric system will be your friend because the amount of salt required can be easily calculated by weighing the water you add when covering your vegetables. Simply weigh your water in grams and multiply that weight by the decimal percentage (e.g., for a 5% brine multiply the weight of water by 0.05). Thus, to make 1,000 g of a 5% brine requires adding 50 g salt, because $0.05 \times 1000 = 50$.

For large batches of pickling—maybe you found lots of stuff you liked at the farmers market or have some especially bountiful plants in the garden at home—consider making a large batch of brine at your preferred strength, maybe a gallon at five percent (a gallon of water will weigh 3,785 g, so you will need to add 189 g salt because $0.05 \times 3,785 = 189$). Extra brine can be kept in jars for the next batch of pickled vegetables.

BASIC FERMENTED PICKLE (CUCUMBERS)

There is so much room for innovation and variety here. Every year I put up a few specific varieties: a nice garlic/dill pickle, a garden herb pickle made with whatever herbs happened to thrive that year (which have included thyme, lemon thyme, oregano, lemon balm, marjoram, and tarragon), and a ghost pepper pickle that scratches my itch for something searing hot and delicious.

Pickling cucumbers are best for pickles. They have thinner skin, are less bitter, and frankly they are just a more convenient size. Pickling cucumbers are available seasonally at farmers markets, and are a bountiful summer crop if you grow two to four plants of a bush variety yourself. Be cautious of grocery-store pickling cucumbers, even more so than other vegetables. Unlike sturdier vegetables such as cauliflower or cabbage, where cucumbers are concerned an extra couple of days spent on a refrigerator truck can mean mushy pickles.

Steer clear of cucumbers that have started to wrinkle or shrivel, and feel for soft spots where the cucumber is bruised.

I often throw some pickling spice into the brine for pickles, using a teaspoon for a quart jar (0.95 L) or a tablespoon for a gallon jug (3.8 L). I add pickling spice into the pot when I am dissolving the salt and calcium chloride. Heating up the pickling spice mixture wakes up the flavors and helps them infuse into the brine. Once the brine cools, I often (but not always) strain out the spices. The spices will continue to add a little flavor if you put them into the fermentation jar, but I prefer not to have to sort through and remove cloves or pieces of bay leaf from my pickle when it is time to eat them. But sometimes I forget to strain the brine and the pickles are none the worse for it.

Pickles also have a few different forms they can take. You can make spears, sliced lengthwise into quarters or eighths. For the last batch or two of the season, I will prepare whole pickles, which will hold up longer. Keeping the cucumber intact slows down the pickling process, as well as the subsequent deterioration. I will also put up a jar or two of slices or chips. This is where a mandolin really comes in handy; it takes very little time to break down a pile of cucumbers into wavy slices that will eventually adorn sandwiches, burgers, or a plate of snacks.

Also be sure to trim the blossom end of the cucumber, that is, the opposite end from the stem. If you are not sure which end that is, it does not hurt to trim a little off both ends. The blossom end contains enzymes that will hasten the breakdown of the cucumber. Evolutionarily, these enzymes help a cucumber to deteriorate and release its seeds into the soil faster, but for home fermenting this will lead to soft and bitter pickles.

Smaller pickling cucumbers, five to six inches (12–15 cm), will have better flavor, texture, and visual appeal than larger ones. As a cucumber gets bigger the inside will start to hollow out, the skin gets thicker, and it will tend to get more bitter.

This method for pickles is also widely applicable to other vegetables. It is your door to a wider world of pickled things. It is a great way to preserve the garlic scapes that briefly appear at the market every year; use them to garnish a Bloody Mary, or mince and add them to a pan sauce or a dressing, or even use a splash of the brine in a garlicky vinaigrette. Radishes work well too, providing a lovely, crunchy topping for tacos or salads, the red outer layer leaching into the brine and coloring the pickled radishes pink. (Larger daikon radishes are also commonly used for kimchi.) Sliced turnips and whole okra are further options.

Cucumber Pickles

Ingredients
- ⦾ 5 pickling cucumbers, trimmed of blossom end, whole, halved, quartered, or sliced
- ⦾ salt, enough for a 5% brine
- ⦾ unchlorinated water
- ⦾ ¼ tsp calcium chloride (optional)
- ⦾ pickling spice (optional)

Directions
1. Pack prepared cucumbers into a half-gallon (1.9 L) jar. Depending on how you break them down, they may or may not fill the jar. Whole cucumbers take up the most space, followed by halves, then quarters, and slices can pack into a jar very efficiently.
2. Top up the jar with water, leaving ¼″ (6 mm) of space at the top. (This volume will reduce slightly in boiling.)
3. Place a pot onto your kitchen scale and zero the scale. Pour the water, but not the cucumbers, into the pot, and measure the weight of the water in grams. Multiply the water weight by 0.05 and add that weight in salt to make a 5% brine. Add calcium chloride and pickling spice, if desired.
4. Boil brine to dissolve salt and calcium chloride. It is not strictly necessary to reach a rolling boil as long as the salt dissolves, but a couple of minutes at a simmer will pull more flavor from the pickling spice, especially if you choose to strain it out.

Putting up a collection of different pickles while the weather is warm helps to preserve part of the summer's bounty and provides a variety of snacking and cooking options.

5. Let brine cool to room temperature and pour over cucumbers. Cover and let sit. After two to three days, you should start seeing some cloudiness, followed by CO_2 bubbles in another day or two. Start tasting at 3–5 days, and move to a refrigerator when the pickles reach the desired sourness.

Embellishments
Optional additions include garlic, dill, peppers, peppercorns, and any number of herbs or spices. The sky is the limit. Want to make pickles flavored with curry powder? Go ahead! Want to make an uber-garlicky pickle with a head (or two heads!) of garlic per quart (approx. a liter)? Go for it! This is where you get to stretch out a bit and test the limits. Create something uniquely your own.

Cucumber Pickles

GREEN BEANS

Pickled green beans are just a timeless classic.

Pickled Green Beans with Fresh Dill

Ingredients

- 250 g green beans, trimmed of stem end
- 15 g bundle of dill, trimmed of thicker stalks
- 3–4 large cloves of garlic, crushed
- 1–2 hot peppers (jalapeno, serrano, cayenne, habanero, it depends on your heat tolerance), halved
- brine, 5%

Directions

Pack beans into a quart or liter jar. Cover with brine and weigh down, leaving an inch or 2–3 cm of headspace. Ferment for a week or two; these are best when the beans are still crisp.

Pickled Green Beans

© Getty/jatrax

PICKLED GARLIC

For this recipe, I prefer to use the garlic with very large cloves that periodically shows up at the grocery store. It is not a flavor thing, I just think it is less work to peel 10 large cloves than 25 small ones. Garlic is pretty pungent on its own, but I have sometimes added mustard seed or pickling spice to my brine at about ½ tsp per pint (475 mL). Cloves of fermented garlic are also a fairly sturdy pickle, so they do not break down very quickly. These will stay good for longer than it takes to use them up. Consider using them in place of fresh garlic for uncooked applications such as aioli or bound salads (i.e., chicken salad, pasta salad, potato salad).

Pickled Garlic Cloves

Ingredients and Directions
- ○ 2 heads' worth of garlic cloves, peeled
- ○ brine, 5%

Directions
Pack cloves into a half-pint or 250 mL jar. Cover with brine. Ferment two to three weeks, or until cloves reach your desired level of acidity, then move to a refrigerator.

NOTE: Fermented garlic may turn a blue or green color due to the formation of pyrroles, which consist of carbon-nitrogen rings. This is the result of a chemical reaction between allicin—the volatile chemical that gives garlic its spicy punch—and the acid formed in the brine during fermentation. When three pyrroles link together, they create a blue coloration; four pyrroles create green (as happens in chlorophyll). Blue or green garlic is perfectly safe to eat. In fact, bright green garlic, known in China as Laba garlic, is produced intentionally for the Chinese New Year. To minimize the likelihood of your pickled garlic turning a startling color, use distilled or carbon-filtered water, which does not contain trace metals; use sea salt or kosher salt, which don't contain iodine; and avoid contact with pots, pans, and utensils made of reactive metals such as aluminum or copper. Limited research on the impact of the age of the garlic has been inconclusive, but young garlic may be less prone to coloring (Laba garlic is aged for months prior to pickling). A quick blanche in boiling water may also help to reduce or eliminate the enzymatic activity that creates the coloration.

PICKLED GARLIC

© Getty/4kodiak

ESCABECHE

As with all of these recipes, the ratio of different vegetables can be adjusted to your tastes. Ten years ago, when I first started making the fermented version of this pickle, it consisted of a lot of carrots, some peppers, and a little onion. Over time, I found that demand for the jalapenos and onions rivaled the carrots, and so the proportions have gradually migrated to a roughly 1:1:1 mix. I like this mix with a slightly stronger brine. Traditionally served alongside a meal in Mexico or available at a certain type of southern California-style Mexican restaurant, it also makes a great addition to tacos, burritos, sandwiches, or just eaten right out of the jar.

Escabeche Pickled Veg

Ingredients
- 10 medium carrots, about 1.5 lb. (650–700 g), cut into 3–4″ (8–10 cm) lengths, then sliced to ¼″ (6 mm) thick
- 10 jalapenos, sliced on the bias
- 2 medium white onions, peel outer layer and trim ends, cut lengthwise (root end to stem) into quarters, then sliced
- brine, 6%

Directions
1. Mix all of the vegetables together in a large bowl. Pack into a half-gallon or 2-liter jar or two quart-sized or 1-liter jars and cover with 6% brine.
2. Ferment for a couple of weeks, until the carrots are fermented all the way through. The carrots will be firm for a while but will eventually soften. The timing on when you move the fermentation to the fridge to slow it down is a matter of preference. Continue to taste this pickle as it ferments; the different flavors are delicious but more distinct when young; they blend and marry the longer the vegetables sit together.

GIARDINIERA

Giardiniera, an Italian tradition, is a great way to use the odds and ends out of your garden, or just mix it up and create something uniquely yours.

Giardiniera literally means "gardener" in Italian. This is less a recipe and more a call to take whatever is fresh from the garden, chop it up, and ferment it into a delicious mix. A perfect third element to go with the meat and cheese on an antipasto plate, it is good enough to share the spotlight, not just play a supporting role. This recipe does not include hot peppers, but you are welcome to punch it up if you like. I have made a batch of a couple of gallons that leaned heavily on cabbage, onions, and serrano peppers. Think of it as a free-form approach to using all the delicious bits of this and that from your garden.

Giardiniera

Ingredients
- 1 medium head cauliflower, trimmed into bite-sized florets
- 2 red bell peppers, cut into slices ½″ wide and 2″ long (approx. 1.5 × 5 cm)
- 2 stalks of celery, sliced into ½″ or 1.5 cm pieces
- 450 g green beans, trimmed of stem end and cut into 2″ or 5 cm lengths
- 3 medium-sized carrots, halved and sliced into ½″ or 1.5 cm pieces
- brine, 5%

Directions

Mix the vegetables together in a large bowl, then pack into a gallon or 4-liter jar. Cover with brine and let ferment 3–4 weeks.

Variations

If you want to take your giardiniera a step further, chop it up to a finer texture, ferment, then put the vegetables into a strainer or colander to drain well, giving it a quick rinse to knock off any residual brine. When your giardiniera is well-drained, pack it into jars with a refined oil and store it in the fridge. To make a Chicago-style giardiniera, use mostly hot peppers with a little finely chopped celery, cauliflower, and carrot, and pack it in oil after fermentation. A more processed oil such as vegetable, canola, or cooking-grade olive oil will remain liquid in the fridge.

If you have not had an oil-packed pickle, it is a revelation. In addition to salty, tangy, and possibly spicy, the fat from the oil enriches the pickle and rounds out the flavor profile. Classically served on an Italian beef sandwich, it is great on anything that benefits from salt, acidity, and fat, which is pretty much everything. Even the oil is gold; one of my go-to methods to roast vegetables is to toss them in some leftover giardiniera oil, cook them in the oven at 425°F (220°C) degrees until they get a nice caramelization, then chop up some giardiniera and mix it in with the roasted vegetables before serving.

CURRIED BRUSSEL SPROUTS

When you look at their resemblance and relationship to cabbage, Brussel sprouts are a natural candidate for fermentation.

Brussel sprouts are essentially tiny cabbages! But just like cabbage, they can have a pretty firm core. Fermentation softens the core up a bit, but if it is still too much for you then consider shredding or slicing them thinly and using them wherever you might use sauerkraut or raw cabbage.

Pickled Curried Brussel Sprouts

Ingredients
- 400 g Brussel sprouts
- 1 tbsp curry powder
- brine, 5%

Directions
1. Trim the ends off of the Brussel sprouts and remove outer leaves. Halve them and pack into a quart or liter canning jar. Sprinkle curry powder over the top and cover with 5% brine.
2. Ferment for at least a couple of weeks to allow curry flavor to fully penetrate the Brussel sprouts. They are sturdy, so they can handle an extended fermentation time.

SAUERKRAUT

Cabbage fermentations can smell and taste unpleasant in the first few days as the fermentation releases sulfur compounds from the cabbage. Give it some time and your fermentation should evolve into a more benign state.

Sauerkraut

Ingredients
- 1 medium head of cabbage, about 1 kg (2.2 lb.)
- salt, 3% by weight of prepared cabbage
- ½ teaspoon dill, caraway, and/or mustard seed (optional)

Directions
1. Trim cabbage of outer leaves. Cut into quarters and remove core. Slice into ribbons about ¼" wide and 2–3 inches long (approx. 0.5 × 5–8 cm). Weigh the prepared cabbage. Multiply the cabbage weight by 0.03 and add that weight in salt. Mix well, and let it weep for a day.
2. If the cabbage does not release enough moisture to cover it in the fermentation vessel, pound the cabbage with a tamper to further break it down. Mix in any optional spices and pack into a crock. Cover with plastic wrap and weigh it down so that the cabbage is below the brine. Many eastern European traditions reserve an outer cabbage leaf to use as a follower, placing it above the kraut and below the weights.
3. Ferment for a few weeks or until your sauerkraut reaches a desired level of acidity, then pack into jars and refrigerate.

WINE-FERMENTED KRAUT

A German tradition that adds another layer of flavor to your sauerkraut.

Wine-Fermented Sauerkraut

Ingredients
- 1 medium head of cabbage, about 1 kg (2.2 lb.)
- salt, 3% by weight of prepared cabbage
- German dry white wine, such as Riesling
- ½ teaspoon dill, caraway, and/or mustard seed (optional)

Directions
1. Trim cabbage of outer leaves. Cut into quarters and remove core. Slice into ribbons about ¼" wide and 2–3" long (approx. 0.5 × 5–8 cm). Weigh the prepared cabbage. Multiply the cabbage weight by 0.03 and add that weight in salt. Mix well, and let it weep for a day.
2. Pack the cabbage along with the liquid into a quart or liter jar or into several pint or half-liter jars. Tamp to pack it down and put a weight on top of your cabbage. Mix in any optional spices and pack into a jar. Pour enough wine over the cabbage to just cover and put a loose lid on your jar.
3. Ferment for a few weeks or until your sauerkraut reaches a desired level of acidity, then refrigerate.

Saurkraut

KIMCHI

Kimchi is a foundational element of Korean food and Korean life. It is so central to Korean dining that appliance companies have produced kimchi fridges that are designed specifically for household kimchi storage. When smiling for a picture, Koreans will say "kimchi" rather than "cheese."

While kimchi has broken more into mainstream American culture in the last ten years, it remains largely a cabbage-based monolith. However, in Korean culture, kimchi encompasses a wide range of ferments—a variety of different vegetables, quick-fermented and long-fermented, mild and spicy.

Chef and cookbook author Edward Lee offers four seasonal varieties in his book *Smoke and Pickles*: a red cabbage and bacon kimchi for the winter, green tomato spring kimchi, white pear summer kimchi, and the commonly-known style of spicy Napa cabbage kimchi for the fall.

Napa cabbage is the variety used for traditional kimchi—the spicy red version that accompanies every Korean meal. But the word "kimchi" is not the name of this one dish only. Rather, think of the word as a verb. You can kimchi anything: cabbage, cucumbers, radishes, oysters, and even fruit.... It is the fermentation that makes it kimchi. I am constantly turning things into kimchi. (Lee 2013, 164)

Lauryn Chun's *The Kimchi Cookbook* includes varieties such as baby spinach and mushroom kimchi, stuffed cucumber kimchi, not to mention a few kimchis based on radishes, green onions, stuffed tomatoes, butternut squash and kale, and seafood. Chun highlights the importance of using different ingredients at different times of the year: "The seasonality of kimchi is integral to its flavors and reflects the vegetables available—warm-weather kimchi is very delicate and light, while cold-weather kimchi's root vegetables are hearty with deep flavors" (Chun 2012, 7).

Chun also echoes Lee in noting that kimchi is as much a method as a recipe. Its name derived from a combination of Chinese characters that mean "salted vegetables" or "soaked vegetables," making kimchi involves four steps: salting (dry or brine), seasoning, fermenting, and storing.

Garlic and ginger often play a prominent role in kimchi, but Korean chile pepper, *gochugaru*, is essential. It is an irreplaceable element in many kimchis, contributing heat and fruitiness to the fermentation. Animal proteins can also play a role in the flavor of kimchi. Seafood products, including dried shrimp, shrimp paste, fish sauce, oysters, squid, or whole fish contribute a pungent, funky savoriness. In some parts of Korea, further from the sea, beef broth is more commonly used to create that savoriness.

Cold-weather kimchis, for eating in the fall and winter, are made with dense vegetables like cabbage and daikon radish that require more time to ferment. These are the kimchis with big, bold flavors that ferment for months and harness what Anthony Bourdain called "the dark forces of rot." They are traditionally fermented in 33-gallon (125 L) clay pots called *onggi*.

Spring and summer kimchis, on the other hand, are a much lesser-known category in the United States. They reflect the seasonality and bounty of the garden and are meant to be eaten

"Best By"

Fermented foods are an excellent example of the vagaries of the "best by" concept. Best-by dates mandated by the US Food and Drug Administration are intended as a quality indicator, not a safety indicator. A best-by date is not a hard-and-fast "expiration" date. That five-year-old can of corned beef in your pantry may no longer be at its peak, but it is not inherently unsafe simply because it is past the best-by date. Given the factors that keep pathogenic microbes at bay—salt, acidity, lack of oxygen—many fermented foods have a very long window of safety. Fully fermented pickles will break down and lose their textural appeal long before they become unsafe to eat. (You might take the opportunity to turn your softening pickles into relish, though.) Moldy cheese merely needs to be trimmed of the mold. Just trust your senses, and do not worry about whether it has been longer than you think something should still be good. Food tends to be very good at letting you know when it has gone bad.

immediately or within a few days. Warm-weather kimchis can be lightly fermented over a day or two, or can be "essentially a dressed salad" (Chun 2012, 30). Water kimchi is a particularly interesting expression, essentially a brothy, tangy, refreshing soup, lightly fermented with small chunks of vegetables. Combined with some cold noodles or rice, it is a bright and easy summer dinner.

Whatever kind of kimchi you make, Chun recommends being flexible and seeing how the flavors develop. Kimchi is constantly evolving and is largely a matter of taste. You can choose to eat a traditionally aged kimchi fresh instead, or you might find that a spring or summer kimchi tastes better after it sits and ferments for a while (Chun 2012, 32).

SPRING ONION KIMCHI

Spring onions make a delicious kimchi (*above*) that can be used fresh or aged for a more robust fermentation flavor (*right*).

Spring onions are traditionally fermented whole for a bright, fresh spring kimchi. I had a bounty of overwintered sweet onions one year, onions that had not been harvested the previous year and had multiplied into small bunches of three or four small onions. I made this recipe when the onions were still golf-ball sized or smaller, using the light green part of the stalk as well (go too far up and it gets fibrous pretty quickly). In the tradition of spring and summer kimchis, this spring onion kimchi is lighter and lower in salt, spice, and intensity. It is delicious in pork lettuce wraps and grain bowls.

Spring Onion Kimchi

Ingredients

- 500 g spring onions, from root to light green part of stem
- 10 g garlic, minced
- 15 g Korean chile powder (gochugaru)
- ¾ tbsp fish sauce
- 16 g salt
- 4 g sugar
- 125 g water

Directions

1. Remove root and outer layer of onions. Slice light green part of stem into ⅛" (3 mm) rounds. Cut onions lengthwise into quarters, then into ⅛" (3 mm) slices.

2. Mix all the ingredients except the water in a large mixing bowl. Pack into a quart or liter jar. Swirl the water in the bowl to pick up any seasoning left behind and pour into jar. Press down the onion to force out air pockets. Ferment at room temperature for 2–3 days, then refrigerate.

GREEN CABBAGE KIMCHI

In the hopes of heading off at least some angry letter-writers, I have to acknowledge first and foremost that I am taking some liberties with this recipe. The biggest liberty is the use of green cabbage. While Napa cabbage is traditional for kimchi, I have come around to the idea of using the denser green cabbage. We prefer it at home because it does not wilt and break down as much; it retains more bite than Napa cabbage, even after several months. In addition, I prefer to cut green cabbage down to ferment into bite-sized pieces.

In Korea, whole or half heads of cabbage would be brined for a day, then painstakingly rubbed down with spice paste between each leaf before the cabbages are packed away to ferment. Cabbage kimchi is traditionally made in November during *kimjang*, the communal process of producing and putting up enormous amounts of kimchi. Kimjang is so important to Korean culture that it is listed as a UNESCO Intangible Cultural Heritage.

I am told that an average of about 150 pounds (40 to 50 cabbage heads) of kimchi per family was made every fall. . . . Making your own batch of kimchi was the only way to ensure that you had an ample supply of vegetables to last you through the winter. (Chun 2012, 62)

There is a tremendous amount of flexibility in this recipe. You can use more or less chile, ginger, garlic, or scallions. You can omit the shrimp paste or swap it out for other options.

Green Cabbage Kimchi

Ingredients

- 1 medium-sized head of cabbage, about 1 kg (2.2 lb.), outer leaves removed, quartered, cored, and cut into 1–1½" (2.5–4 cm) pieces
- 1 large carrot, shredded
- 40 g Korean chile flakes (gochugaru)
- 25 g ginger, minced
- 25 g garlic, minced
- 8 scallions, trimmed and sliced into thin rounds
- 4 tsp sugar
- 10 g shrimp paste, several dashes of fish sauce, or a few spoonfuls of dried anchovies (all optional)
- 50 g salt
- 150 mL unchlorinated water

Directions

1. Toss the prepared cabbage with salt, then pound for a few minutes with a wooden tamper or other tool to help break up the cabbage so that it releases moisture. Let sit for several hours or overnight.

2. Add all remaining ingredients to a bowl. Mix well with the cabbage and make sure the seasonings are well-distributed on the cabbage pieces. Pack into a quart or liter jar or a couple of pint or half-liter jars. Add 150 mL water to the bowl and scrape up any residual seasonings. Top up the jars with this extra water and weigh down the cabbage mixture so that it sits below the brine level.

3. Ferment for a couple of weeks or longer, to taste, then refrigerate. As noted in the sauerkraut recipe, your cabbage fermentation may get funky for a few days as the fermentation blows off sulfur compounds from the cabbage, but this stage will pass.

Kimchi

© Getty/WRS Photos

5

HOT SAUCE, SALSA, RELISH, AND CHUTNEY

People on every continent have found ways to spice up their foods. Residues of herbs and spices have been identified in food containers that date back as far as 6,000 years. For millennia, spices and other pungent ingredients were used both as medicine and to cover the general smell of unwashed people and open sewers. Two thousand years ago, the Romans were salting fish for a savory, protein-rich fish sauce called *garum*. Domesticated chiles go back thousands of years, as do most of the pungent go-to spices from cuisines around the world.

> Up until a few thousand years ago, your choice of spice had everything to do with the continent you called home. If you lived in Europe, it was mustard and horseradish. If you lived in Asia, you used either black pepper and its relatives or ginger. . . . If you lived in the Americas, your go-to spice was the chile. (Shockey and Shockey 2017, 4)

The worldwide spice trade introduced peppercorns, ginger, mustard, and many other ingredients to new cultures (and created vast wealth for those who controlled the movement of spices). Over centuries, flavors from Asia, the Middle East, Africa, and the Western Hemisphere crisscrossed the globe. Chile peppers were picked up in the New World by Europeans around 1500 and quickly worked their way into food traditions around the world.

Spices have a well-documented preservative effect on food, helping protect against spoilage microbes as well as pathogenic ones. They have antioxidative properties, largely due to the presence of phenolic compounds that reduce lipid oxidation, also known as rancidity. A wide variety of whole spices and their essential oils have also been shown to have a wide range of antimicrobial effects, reducing the growth of bacteria, yeasts, and molds (Gottardi 2016, 6–13).

A 1998 study in the *Quarterly Review of Biology* examined the use of 43 spices in 36 different countries, using 4,578 meat-based recipes from 93 traditional cookbooks, to show that countries with a hotter climate—where levels of microbial growth are higher—relied on cuisines with high levels of spicing to reduce spoilage and pathogenic growth. The authors found their data did not support the alternative possibilities that the spices provided macronutrients, disguised the taste and smell of food that had spoiled, increased perspiration in the eater and thus helped people to stay cool, or potentially had no benefit. They concluded that a taste for spices offered an evolutionary benefit:

> *The proximate reason spices are used obviously is to enhance food palatability. But the ultimate reason is most likely that spices help cleanse foods of pathogens and thereby contribute to the health, longevity and reproductive success of people who find their flavors enjoyable.* (Billing and Sherman 1998, 3)

There is also a synergistic effect from using multiple spices. That 1998 study also found that recipes from hotter countries and regions generally contained more spices and spices with more potent antibacterial effects (e.g., cinnamon, cumin, onion, garlic, and chile peppers) than foods from cooler areas (Billing and Sherman 1998, 21).

Fermented condiments such as mustard, hot sauce, salsa, relish, and chutney are a natural extension of the fermented vegetable process. For hot sauces and salsas, I prefer to ferment the vegetables in a brine (p. 55), then break them down in a food processor. Relishes and chutneys, on the other hand, do not get brine-fermented before being processed. Instead, they get broken down, seasoned, and packed to ferment.

Sometimes when making brine-fermented vegetables, it might seem like you are using an excessive amount of salt, but most of it will be left behind in brine that is not consumed. For chopped, mixed pickles such as relish, the final

amount of salt is added into the mix. Salt is generally added at a rate of 3%–5%; you can go lower or higher to taste, but condiments should be well-seasoned.

From gochujang in Korea, to sambal in southeast Asia, harissa in northern Africa, sauces featuring habaneros and Scotch bonnets in the Caribbean, to cayenne-based hot sauces in North America, there are countless varieties of hot sauces around the world. Some are pure fermentations of salt, chiles, and maybe a splash of water. Others are complex medleys of peppers and spices. They can be thick or thin, stabilized with vinegar or not.

Commercial examples of fermented hot sauce include Tabasco (which has vinegar added back to the fermented mash), as well as sriracha and sambal. The method is simple enough: ferment your peppers of choice—and optionally some onion, garlic, or other seasonings of choice (citrus zest, coriander, cumin, ginger, lemongrass, and black pepper are good options)—for a couple of weeks up to a few months for increased complexity. Strain out the peppers and other vegetables and puree them to your preferred thickness, possibly adding back some of the brine to loosen up the sauce, or vinegar to increase the long-term stability of the sauce.

Fresno peppers, shown here after fermentation, make an excellent hot sauce. They are similar in heat to jalapeños but provide a mild fruitiness and slight smokiness.

Hot sauce and salsa are variations on the same theme. *Salsa* does, after all, mean "sauce." For hot sauce and salsa fermentations, peppers should be halved to facilitate the fermentation process.

Other vegetables need to be cut down into manageable pieces, but do not worry about making them perfectly consistent. If pieces are relatively close in size they will ferment at the same rate, but in the long run they are all going into a blender.

Along with its obvious uses, salsa is a great way to augment your slow cooker experience. A couple of chicken breasts or a piece of tough, flavorful beef (chuck or bottom round are good), some vegetables (carrots, onions, potatoes, mushrooms, garlic, in whatever proportions suit you), a splash of broth, and a cup or two of salsa can make a great meal.

To reduce heat in favor of flavor in your pepper sauces (your less-hot sauce), remove both the seeds *and* the ribs from some or all of the peppers you are using. If you want to just temper it a little, start by deseeding and de-ribbing a quarter or half of your peppers. If you are really looking to focus on flavor without heat, then go for it and remove seeds and ribs from all of them.

Keep in mind that you are rolling the capsaicin dice no matter what you do. While general guidelines for heat are reliable (i.e., bell pepper < jalapeño < habanero), there can be enormous variety from one pepper to another, one crop to another, one field to another. The amount and timing of water that a chile pepper plant receives is an enormous factor in how much capsaicin is produced in the fruit of the plant.

Always wear gloves when handling chile peppers. When washing utensils, cutting boards, and food processor parts, begin with cold water to knock off any solids before using hot water to wash. If you start with hot water, it will volatilize the capsaicin and, depending on the type of peppers, you may find yourself in a coughing fit while standing over the sink.

RECIPES

As you saw for the pickle and sauerkraut recipes in chapter 4, brine is a necessary element in these recipes. Brine solutions can be made a certain percentage strength by weighing the water you use and calculating the necessary salt (see p. 55). For some recipes, such as this one, the water is considered an ingredient and included when calculating the salt addition.

HOMEMADE FERMENTED MUSTARD

This is not the yellow mustard you might be used to. The ground mustard seed (Coleman's is a commonly available brand) packs some punch, similar to the spice that horseradish has.

Homemade, fermented mustard, with its horseradish-y bite, is a very different condiment from the vinegary yellow stuff commonly used on hot dogs and hamburgers.

Fermented Mustard

Ingredients
- ○ 50 g whole mustard seed (yellow, brown, black, or a combination)
- ○ 60 g ground mustard seed
- ○ 7.8 g salt
- ○ 150 g water
- ○ Herbs, garlic, chiles, or chile powder (all optional)

Directions
Pound the mustard seeds lightly in a mortar and pestle, just to break them open. Mix all ingredients in a pint jar. Cover jar with a lid and let ferment for a couple of weeks, then put into the fridge.

HABANERO HOT SAUCE

Habanero peppers have a wonderful tropical fruitiness, but they can also be a palate-searing experience. This is an unabashedly *hot* sauce. Depending on your heat preference, consider removing the seeds and ribs from some or all of the habanero peppers. Try adding some lime zest or lemongrass to this recipe for an added dimension.

Habaneros bring a wonderful tropical flavor, and plenty of heat, to fermented hot sauce.

Habanero Hot Sauce

Ingredients
- 12 habaneros, stemmed and halved
- 1 large carrot, cut roughly into chunks
- 2 cloves garlic, halved
- ¼ small white onion, roughly sliced
- ½ tsp coriander seed
- brine, 6%, to cover

Directions
1. Ferment the vegetables together in a quart or liter jar for at least a month. It will take time for the carrot to fully ferment and soften.
2. When fermentation is complete, strain the vegetables from the brine and put into a blender. Puree until smooth. For a thinner sauce, add back in some brine to reach desired consistency.

Habanero Hot Sauce

© Getty/Marcos Elihu Castillo Ramirez

RED BELL PEPPER SAUCE

This stuff is really versatile, something that started off with garlic, olive oil and red bell peppers and has evolved over the years, becoming something that has worked its way into regular usage at home. It is a great condiment for sandwiches, or to bake chicken breasts in (maybe with some green olives and baby potatoes). Mix in some tomatoes and use it as the base for a pasta sauce. Smear it on a piece of flatbread or pizza dough in lieu of tomato sauce, throw on your preferred cheese and toppings, and bake a delicious—if slightly untraditional—pizza.

Red Bell Pepper Sauce

Ingredients
- 4 red bell peppers
- 6 cloves roasted garlic
- brine, 5%, to cover

Directions
Ferment for two weeks to a couple of months, as desired. Strain out peppers and garlic, puree together until smooth. Pack in a pint or half-liter jar and refrigerate.

SALSA VERDE

Fermentation is a delicious way to add another layer of flavor to salsas, and helps to keep them more biologically stable when stored in the fridge.

Salsa Verde

Ingredients
- 18 tomatillos, halved
- 9 small serrano peppers, halved (you could also substitute three or four jalapeños)
- 6 cloves garlic, smashed
- 1 white onion, coarsely chopped
- ¼ tsp Mexican oregano
- ½ tsp ground cumin
- brine, 5%, to cover

Directions
Ferment the vegetables together in a half-gallon or two-liter jar for two weeks to a couple of months, as desired. Strain out vegetables and puree together until smooth. Pack in pint or half-liter jars and refrigerate.

DILL RELISH

If you have some extra pickling cucumbers that you do not know what to do with, or maybe you already have jars of pickles stacked to the ceiling, you can practice your knife skills and make some dill relish.

Cucumber Relish with Dill

Ingredients
- ○ 2 pickling cucumbers, minced
- ○ 3–4 sprigs of dill, chopped finely
- ○ 1 clove garlic (optional), minced
- ○ salt, 3% by weight of other ingredients

Directions
1. Mix cucumber, dill, and garlic in a bowl. Weigh this mixture in grams. Multiply that weight by 0.03 and add that amount of salt in grams. Let sit for a couple of hours to allow the salt to pull moisture out of the vegetables.
2. Pack into pint or half-pint (500 or 250 mL) jars and put a weight on the mixture to press the relish below the liquid level.
3. Ferment for 2–3 weeks.

Cucumber Relish

© Getty/Mariha-kitchen

MIXED RELISH

You can make a relish with whatever good things come out of the garden. In this case, it was a small sweet onion, a couple of banana peppers, a cucumber, some lemon thyme and oregano, and a flowering head of dill fronds. (When my dill started bolting, I did not worry about it. I just started substituting the big flowering heads, along with the nascent dill seeds, into my pickles. The flavor is not exactly the same, but similar and delicious in its own right.) Adapt this to whatever your garden offers; it is a concept as much as a recipe.

Mixed Relish

Ingredients
- ○ 1 pickling cucumber, minced
- ○ 2 banana peppers, chopped finely
- ○ 1 small onion, chopped finely
- ○ 2–3 sprigs lemon thyme, leaves only
- ○ salt, 3% by weight of other ingredients
- ○ 1–2 heads dill flowers

Directions
1. Mix cucumber, peppers, onion, and thyme in a bowl. Weigh this mixture in grams. Multiply that weight by 0.03 and add that amount of salt in grams. Let sit for a couple hours to allow the salt to pull moisture out of the vegetables.
2. Put the flowering heads of dill into pint or half-pint (500 or 250 mL) jars, pack the relish in on top, and put a weight on the mixture to press the relish below the liquid level.
3. Ferment for 2–3 weeks. Remove the heads of dill before using.

JALAPEÑO CORN RELISH

Jalapeño Corn Relish

Ingredients
- 6 minced jalapeños
- 2 ears of corn
- 90 g white onion, chopped
- 1 clove garlic, minced
- ⅛ tsp cumin
- ¼ tsp oregano
- salt, 3% by weight of other ingredients

Directions
1. Roast the corn on a grill to develop gently charred spots. Cut the kernels off of the ears and add to a mixing bowl. Add jalapeño, onion, and seasonings to the bowl. Weigh all ingredients. Weigh this mixture in grams. Multiply that weight by 0.03 and add that amount of salt in grams. Let sit for a couple of hours to allow the salt to pull moisture out of the vegetables.
2. Pack the relish into a half-pint or 250 mL jar. Add a weight on top to push down vegetables below the liquid level, adding a splash of lime juice if necessary.
3. Ferment for 2–3 weeks.

Variations
This recipe is also excellent with two or three roasted Pueblo, Hatch, or Anaheim green chile peppers substituted for the jalapeños.

A mix of peppers and fire-roasted corn makes a delicious relish.

MANGO CHUTNEY

Fermented mango, raisin, chile pepper, and spices make a delicious chutney.

Mango Chutney

Ingredients
- 1 mango, chopped (about 300 g)
- 20 g raisins, chopped
- 1 serrano pepper, minced
- 1 clove garlic, minced (about 3 g)
- Small piece of ginger, minced (about 5 g)
- ½ tsp turmeric, minced (about 1.5 g)
- salt, 3% by weight of other ingredients
- brown sugar, 1% by weight of other ingredients

Directions
1. Mix mango, raisins, pepper, garlic, ginger, and turmeric together in a bowl. Weigh all ingredients in grams. First, multiply the ingredients' weight by 0.03 and add that amount of salt in grams; second, multiply the ingredients' weight by 0.01 and add that amount of brown sugar in grams. Let sit for a few hours to allow the salt and sugar to draw moisture out of the mango.
2. Pack the mixture into a jar, pressing down hard to try to submerge as much of the mixture as possible. Add a weight to keep the chutney mixture down, adding a splash of water or lemon juice as necessary to cover the chutney.
3. Ferment for a few days at room temperature and transfer to the refrigerator when it reaches your desired level of fermentation, which may be before all of the fruit sugars have been fermented.

Mango Chutney

6

DAILY

Cheesemaking is an ancient practice that may go back as far as the domestication of livestock 10,000 years ago. At some point, humans learned that enzymes present in an animal stomach reacted with milk to congeal and separate the fat and some of the protein (the curd) from the watery liquid left behind (the whey). It is easy to imagine a farmer or shepherd out in the field thousands of years ago, carrying their daily portion of milk in a dried stomach and finding it has curdled, leading to the discovery of rudimentary cheese. If you add to that process salting and acidification through bacterial action, both of which help create firmer, more distinct curds and help create a hospitable environment to important flavor-enhancing microbes, then you are not far from some modern cheeses. The process results in a condensed product that preserves milk solids in a more stable form, in "an intense, concentrated expression of pastures and animals, of microbes and time" (McGee 2004, 51).

There are thousands of different types of cheeses and other fermented dairy products around the world, from simple soured milks to giant wheels of cheese aged in caves for years. Most food cultures outside of East Asia rely on dairy as a staple, and wherever there is dairy, there is fermented dairy. Sandor Katz noted how there is an inherent aspect of *terroir* in many cheeses made around the world. This concept comes from the tradition of French winemaking, which holds that the location and environment that ingredients come from have an impact on flavor:

> The context for cheesemaking goes beyond the social to the biological. All the varied cheesemaking traditions developed out of particular environmental factors, specifically the varied climates and terrains favorable to different animals and producing very different milks, and the varied microorganisms present in the milk and aging environments in different places. (Katz 2012, 206)

The first industrial cheesemaking factory did not open until 1815 in Switzerland, with the first American factory opening in New York in 1851. Along with so many other aspects of food production, cheesemaking was moved from the farm to the factory during the rapid industrialization of the nineteenth and twentieth centuries, becoming a standardized, commoditized product. (Prices for cheese in America as a commodity are set according to the price for a 40-pound block of cheddar, with other bulk cheeses priced in relation to that benchmark.) Since the rise of the back-to-the-land social movement in the 1970s, along with the fact that the world is getting smaller and access to fantastic cheeses from around the world has broadened Americans' view of what cheese can be, a growing number of small American cheesemakers have been pushing craft in place of commodity.

The farmstead and artisanal cheesemakers of the late twentieth century through today have once again embraced local and regional production, making unique cheeses with local milk. They can now fill entire displays at your local grocer. Even my city of less than 100,000 people has a store largely dedicated to artisanal cheeses from around the world. As an aside: if you do not know what kind of cheese you want to make, stores that sell artisanal cheeses are a great place to start tasting and exploring.

As food fermentations go, the transition from milk to cheese is one of the more dramatic transformations. There is something magical about how, "through a series of manipulations, you transform fluid milk into a solid block of concentrated flavor" (Katz 2012, 202).

A wide variety of milks have been used by humankind over thousands of years, but the most commonly available in the United States are cow's milk and, a distant second, goat's milk. Either one can be used for the recipes in this chapter, as can more exotic dairy options. Non-dairy "milks," such as soy or almond milk, will not work the same way, which is one reason you do not see blocks of soy-milk cheddar cheese in stores.

Cow and goat milks consist of about 12% milk solids, which includes protein, fat, lactose (milk sugar), and other components, with water making up the remainder. Cheesemaking is the process of coagulating the protein casein to form curds. Casein makes up about 3% of the milk. The curds retain most of the fat, known as butterfat, which makes up about 4% of the original milk weight, while lactose accounts for 4%–5%.

Water, the primary component of milk, weighs 8.34 pounds per gallon (in metric, this translates to 1,000 g, or 1 kg, per liter). Because hard cheeses such as cheddar or Parmesan lose almost all of their water through cutting, cooking, pressing, and aging, a gallon of milk will yield about a pound of hard cheese (or 1 L of milk yields about 120 g of cheese). The more whey is removed, the firmer and more shelf-stable the cheese will be, and the lower the yield. Soft cheeses such as chevre retain about 50% whey, so these cheeses yield about two pounds of cheese per gallon (240 g per liter). Soft cheeses are easier to produce but have a more limited shelf life and are best consumed young.

These numbers are approximations and will vary based on the type and breed of animal, small differences in cheesemaking techniques, even differences in types of feed and pasture. Sheep's milk, if you can find it, tends to be very high yielding, more than twice the previously noted amounts. However, the sheep themselves yield less milk, so expect to pay much more per gallon.

Cow's milk also contains varying levels of carotene in the butterfat, which can lead to the traditional yellow-orange color of cheeses such as cheddar and Colby. Grass-fed cows and some breeds like Jersey tend to have much more carotene in their milk, which will naturally be more yellow-orange. The color of these cheeses became falsely associated with quality and led to industrial-scale practices of adding color. Most commercial examples of these cheeses in America are now colored with annatto to compensate for changes in the cows' diet that lead to less carotene and help the color of the product remain consistent year-round, but some of the best cheddars in the world are a creamy white. Goat's milk contains no carotene, so goat's milk cheeses will always be white.

Goat's milk has a sharpness compared to cow's milk, which is the result of the presence of the enzyme lipase. If you are fond of the unique character of goat's milk but cannot source it, powdered lipase can be added to cow's milk to approximate that flavor. Goat's milk, unlike cow's milk, is also naturally homogenized. This leads to a slightly softer cheese and a softer curd.

Raw or unhomogenized cow's milk, on the other hand, will separate into a layer of cream on top and lower-fat milk below that. Skimming that cream off will leave you with the original, literal, "skim" milk, which can be used to ferment as-is, enrich another cheese, or drink. Crème fraîche is a rich, thick product that results from cream fermented for a day or two; if this fermented cream is churned or agitated it will separate into cultured butter and buttermilk. (Grocery store buttermilk, or "cultured buttermilk," is a different product, made from pasteurized milk with a bacterial culture added back in.)

It is also crucial to NOT use ultrapasteurized milk, as the high temperatures used in that process will inhibit curd formation afterwards. Many commercial milks available in the grocery store have been subjected to ultrapasteurization to increase shelf life, so check labels on the milk you choose. Homogenized and regular pasteurized milk is OK to use, but use calcium chloride to help with firmer curd formation.

The type of cheese is not necessarily defined by the type of milk, though many cheeses have a specific type of milk that is traditionally required. Whatever milk you use, the fresher you can get it the better your cheese will be, and animals raised on a traditional diet will provide a better flavor than milk from feed-lot animals raised on corn. Some rennet adjustments may need to be made when substituting types of milk (sheep's milk will need slightly less rennet than cow's milk, goat's milk will need slightly more), but follow the recipe the first time through, take good notes, and hold off making any changes until your second batch. As any good artisanal producer will tell you, record-keeping is crucial to develop consistency and to understand how small variables affect your final product.

CULTURES

Bacterial and mold starters are the acidifying and flavor-developing cultures that get added to the milk. Lactic-acid bacteria consume lactose in the milk and convert it to lactic acid, which helps the curds to coagulate and acts as a preservative. Starters can be "direct-set"—essentially a fresh batch of freeze-dried bacteria for every batch of cheese—or a starter recultured from a previous batch or from yogurt with live cultures. For thousands of years, before the isolation of specific bacterial and mold strains, continuous propagations were traditional in cheesemaking, where part of the previous batch of cheese was used to inoculate the next batch. Because of the potential inconsistencies and difficulties in maintaining a culture, all of the recipes in this book call for direct-set cultures.

There are a wide variety of microbes that can be called upon depending on the cheese being made. The two main different types of cheese cultures are mesophilic and thermophilic. Mesophilic cheese cultures prefer a lower ripening temperature, roughly 85°F (29°C). Mesophilic cheeses include cheddar, Colby, blue, and Monterey Jack. Thermophilic cultures are more active at a higher temperature, preferring about 110°F (43°C). Thermophilic cheeses include mozzarella, provolone, Swiss, and Parmesan. Both types of culture have a roughly 40-degree Fahrenheit window of activity (or a 22-degree Celsius window) centered around the ideal temperature, so you may see recipes call for temperatures that are a little higher or lower than optimal. You also may be able to salvage a cheese if you find your ripening temperature is off the mark.

The cultures active in yogurt are generally a mix of *Lactobacillus delbrueckii* subsp.

bulgaricus and *Streptococcus salivarius* subsp. *thermophilius*. The presence of these bacteria together helps stimulate the growth of the other, and their combined activity acidifies the milk more rapidly than either species would on its own (McGee 2004, 48). Sour cream and butter are primarily *Lactococcus* and *Leuconostoc* species, both of which are diacetyl producers. (Diacetyl is a buttery-tasting compound, considered an off-flavor in beer fermentation but synthesized to produce "butter flavor" for movie theater popcorn.) Kefir is an increasingly popular dairy product, a soured dairy drink that is fermented by kefir "grains," which are a symbiotic, multi-culture inoculant.

Additional cultures important for cheesemaking include *Propionibacter freudenreichii* subsp. *shermanii* (generally sold as *Propionibacter shermanii*), which creates the carbon dioxide bubbles or holes in Swiss and Emmenthaler; *Brevibacterium linens*, which gives red-mold cheeses such as Époisses or Limburger their color and trademark funk; *Penicillium roqueforti*, which gives blue cheeses their veins and traditional sharp flavor; and *Penicillium camemberti*, which imbues traditional surface-ripened cheeses such as Brie or Camembert with their soft paste and mushroomy, earthy flavors. Some cultures may create enzymes that slowly turn your cheese into an oozy, funky paste, or facilitate the slow transformation of milk proteins into savory compounds. There are potentially infinite combinations of single or mixed cultures, plus different types of milk, as well as environmental factors. As French statesman Charles de Gaulle famously lamented, "How can you govern a country that has 246 varieties of cheese?"

COAGULANTS

All cheeses are coagulated in some fashion. In some cases, an acidic ingredient such as citrus juice, vinegar, or citric acid will both acidify the milk and, at high temperatures, coagulate the milk. This method is used for simple, fast cheeses such as queso fresco or farmer's cheese. An acid will begin to thicken milk at about pH 4.6.

Most cultured cheeses use rennet for a coagulant. Rennet is a naturally occurring mix of enzymes found in the fourth stomach of a calf. The active enzymes, chymosin (rennin) and pepsin, act on the milk protein casein, causing it to coagulate into a soft, gelatinous mass that contains the butterfat and some of the whey. While a high-acidity environment will make milk curdle quickly, a lower dosage of starter culture—which acidifies milk and encourages curdling on its own—plus rennet is more effective than acidity alone and allows for greater bacterial flavor development. Rennet is active between 50°F and 130°F (10–54°C), overlapping with the temperature ranges of both mesophilic and thermophilic cheese cultures.

Rennet is made traditionally from calf stomachs as a byproduct of the veal industry, or, more recently, from engineered bacterial cells that have the gene for chymosin inserted into their DNA, allowing them to produce a substitute rennet in place of calf rennet. There is also vegetable rennet available, derived from a mold (*Rhizomucor miehei*). Nettles and thistles also provide a similar coagulation capacity, though long-aged cheeses made with vegetarian rennet are said to develop a hint of bitterness.

Rennet comes in two forms, liquid and tablet. I personally prefer liquid rennet for its ease of use. Rennet is used in very small amounts, often measured in drops or fractions of a teaspoon per gallon, so it is much easier to measure out the proper dosage in liquid form than to cut up precise portions of a rennet tablet. Additionally, liquid rennet needs to be diluted in water to ensure proper distribution otherwise it can result in uneven curdling. Be sure that, whatever your water source is, you are using unchlorinated water, because chlorine can interfere with rennet and coagulation. It is also important to check that your milk does not contain stabilizers or thickeners, which, similarly, can interfere with protein coagulation.

SALT

Salt is an essential ingredient in cheesemaking—important for flavor, texture, and stability—and a wide range of other food fermentations. Because of its importance in so many different ferments, I have dedicated an appendix to the subject (p. 145).

STAGES

Basic cheesemaking can be divided into a few distinct stages: ripening, cutting curds, and draining and molding. You can age your cheese too, though this is optional.

RIPENING

In the ripening stage, the milk is heated to the inoculation temperature and bacterial starters work alongside the coagulant to acidify the milk and separate the curds and whey. The milk must be heated gently to prevent harming the proteins in the milk and making them grainy. It helps to take the milk out of the fridge and let it come to room temperature while you are preparing your equipment, reviewing the recipe and your notes, and getting yourself in the right frame of mind with a little snack of cheese.

I generally use gentle direct heating on the stovetop with a heavy-duty Dutch oven to make cheese. A Dutch oven heats slowly and evenly and retains heat well. As long as you keep the heat low and periodically stir to ensure even heating, you run little risk of damaging the milk. A hot-water bath or double boiler—keeping the milk pot inside of a larger pot of water on the stove—is both a gentle way to heat the cheese and an excellent way to retain heat during ripening.

The preheating stage is also a good moment to add calcium chloride if using store-bought pasteurized homogenized milk. Because it comes in crystalline form, calcium chloride needs to dissolve to be effective, so be sure to stir it in and feel for graininess at the bottom of the pot. Alternatively, dissolve the calcium chloride in a little non-chlorinated water, stir well, and then stir it into the milk.

The culture and rennet additions are carefully calibrated for a specific amount of milk at a specific temperature, creating a controlled process so that acidification proceeds at the same pace as coagulation. Many cheesemaking recipes in this book and elsewhere will call for the addition of the culture, followed by a rest period, then the addition of the rennet. Other recipes will call for both additions at the same time.

When the culture is added to the milk, allow it to sit and hydrate for a few minutes. This will help it to better mix into the milk evenly without clumping up. Once you are ready to mix the culture, it is important to whisk in an up-and-down motion to ensure proper dispersion. Simply stirring in a circular motion can lead to uneven pockets of milk without culture, especially in the bottom of the pot. The same applies when adding rennet, which should be prediluted to help it to disperse evenly through the milk. Stirring after the curd has begun to set will weaken the curd and cause loss of butterfat, giving a drier cheese. Relative to cow's milk, goat's milk will be more acidic and faster ripening, with more delicate curds that must be treated carefully.

CUTTING CURDS

Once the curd forms a clean break from the whey, becoming a soft but cohesive mass that has separated from the whey and can be cut cleanly with a curd knife, thermometer, or other straight

After coagulating and knitting into a cohesive mat, cheese curds often need to be cut into smaller pieces (*left*) so that the curds will exude more whey and become firmer (*right*).

but dull instrument, it can be cut to encourage the whey to drain out and the curds to consolidate. Waiting too long will give a curd that is too firm; the process will break the curd rather than cutting it.

For the soft cheese recipes featured here, cutting is a process of skimming off half-inch-thick layers of curd with a mesh ladle and gently putting them into a cheesecloth-lined colander to drain. These curds will be very delicate and will retain more moisture in the final cheese, resulting in a soft cheese rather than a hard cheese.

For other cheeses, cutting involves cubing the curd and allowing it to drain further in the whey. When you are ready to cut the curd, once it gives a clean break, the first step is to cut vertically through the curd in ½" (1.25 cm) increments. Turn the pot 90° and repeat the vertical cuts, giving you ½" (1.25 cm) square curds. Turn the pot again and, rather than cutting vertically, angle your curd knife 45° and cut again at ½" increments. Turn the pot once more and cut again at diagonal ½" increments.

Gently stir the curds, which will be very delicate still, to check for large masses of curd that did not get cut.

After cutting, curds are often left to rest at a higher temperature, and should be periodically stirred to keep them from matting and to help expel whey. Some milder cheeses, like Gouda, Havarti, and Monterey Jack, also use a curd-washing method, where whey is removed and water is added. This will pull lactose out of the curds, leading to lower acidity in the final cheese.

DRAINING AND MOLDING

For very soft cheeses, draining the curds involves tying the cheesecloth at the top after the liquid has drained out, and hanging to finish draining at room temperature into a pot or a sink. A longer hanging time will produce a drier and more acidic cheese. Salt can be gently mixed in at this time. The curds could be packed into a plastic mold to determine the shape of the cheese; soft cheeses can also be stored unshaped in covered plastic or glass containers.

Draining Whey

Many soft cheeses require time hanging to drain whey, allowing the curds to consolidate. © *Getty Images Plus*

Hard cheeses are generally cut and allowed to drain, then salted and pressed (or pressed and brined). The salt helps to draw out moisture and consolidate the curds, as well as acting as a preservative. That's not all salt does, as Mary Karlin explains in *Artisan Cheese Making at Home*:

Salt contributes to surface dehydration and rind formation; it deactivates the cultures and stops the acidification process; it slows the aging process so cheese can be held long enough to develop the desired texture; and it enhances the inherent flavors by affecting the formation of flavor compounds in the cheese.
(Karlin 2011, 14)

Avoid salts that have been iodized, because this can inhibit bacterial action, and have other additives such as anticaking agents. Expensive, boutique salts are not necessary either. I have always been comfortable with sea salt, cheese salt, or kosher salt, using all three with no ill effects.

Some cheeses require curds to be separated into a mold to be shaped and pressed to remove whey.

Pressing the cheese helps to expel additional whey, creating a denser product. None of the cheeses in this book require a press, but a variety of options, from fully assembled to build-it-yourself, are available.

AGING (OPTIONAL)
Hard cheeses are aged using a combination of temperature and humidity that allows for the slow development of flavor. Rind development is an important factor in aging cheese.

When a cheese ages, it creates two separate environments: the paste, which is internal, and the rind, which is external. If the moisture level is too high, it will encourage mold growth on the rind, and if the moisture is too low, it will result in a brittle, cracked rind. Some cheeses are washed regularly, or waxed to protect them; some are smeared with additional bacteria, still others have molds that are encouraged to grow on the surface. Depending on the cheese, aging can extend for weeks in the case of mold-ripened cheeses like Brie, or up to years for a large, dense wheel of Parmesan that is full of savory character as a result of the slow enzymatic breakdown of proteins and fat.

ON RAW MILK AND PASTEURIZATION
Federal safety regulations concerning raw milk can be a sore spot with cheesemakers. In the United States, commercial cheeses made from raw milk must be aged at least 60 days to ensure safety. This law precludes fresh cheeses from being made with raw milk and, hence, has become a point of contention with some artisanal cheesemakers, as well as with cheese afficionados who have experienced amazing raw-milk cheeses in other countries. A few European countries, by comparison, prohibit the use of pasteurized milk in some of the world's great cheeses, such as French *appellation d'origine contrôlée* (AOC) Brie or Italian Parmigiano-Reggiano.

This does not prohibit the home cheesemaker from using raw milk, if they can find it. Laws concerning raw milk vary from state to state—running the gamut from where it can be purchased in a store, on the farm, exclusively via a cow-share program, or where it is outright illegal—and the US Food and Drug Administration prohibits the interstate sale of any unpasteurized milk. I have purchased it from a small family farm whose safety and quality I knew was excellent, and seen raw milk of unknown legality sell for exorbitant prices at a farmer's market in a cow-share state.

At the turn of the twentieth century, as America was in the throes of industrialization, milk was being transported farther and farther under questionable conditions to be distributed widely in the booming cities. Raw milk became a significant disease vector, accounting for a large percentage of food and waterborne illnesses. Pasteurization, developed by Louis Pasteur in 1862, offered a method to kill potentially dangerous microbes, and first became mandatory in Chicago in 1908. In 1947 Michigan became the first state to mandate pasteurization, and by the early 1970s the FDA was working to limit access to raw milk.

Even proponents of raw milk, such as Sandor Katz, concede that pasteurization is recommended for milk that comes from industrial operations:

> Animals in the large "farms" known as concentrated animal feeding operations (CAFO) do not enjoy the same health as animals allowed to roam and graze. Nor does their milk possess the same qualities. If we must drink the milk of these animals, it is safest pasteurized, due to high somatic cell (pus in the milk, from udder stress) and coliform bacteria counts. But let's not extrapolate from that unfortunate reality. . . . Change the context, by providing animals with space to roam and graze and raw milk can certainly be safe, not to mention delicious, nutritious, digestible, and rich in healthful and self-protective lactic acid bacteria. (Katz 2012, 184)

While pasteurization is an important way to destroy dangerous pathogens that may be in milk, including salmonella and *E. coli*, it also degrades vitamins, useful enzymes, beneficial bacteria, texture, and flavor (Karlin 2011, 10). The process denatures 4%–7% of the milk proteins, generating a slightly weaker curd. Both pasteurization and homogenization remove calcium or render it insoluble. This slows down the action of rennet but can be remedied with a pinch of calcium chloride, available at most homebrew stores or online cheese shops.

It is also important to consider that, while raw milk today may be exponentially safer than it was 100 years ago, CDC statistics indicate that raw milk and raw-milk cheeses make up 96% of all dairy-related illnesses. And keep in mind that all of the fresh cheeses and dairy products you have legally purchased in the United States are made from pasteurized milk. Using raw milk, if it is even available, is a risk–reward calculation that the home cheesemaker has to work out for themselves.

If you have any doubts or concerns about the safety of your raw milk, go ahead and pasteurize it. Pasteurization operates on a sliding scale, with shorter times required at higher temperatures, but Ricki Carroll recommends operating on the low end of the spectrum, 145°F (63°C) for 30 minutes with a rapid cool down in an ice bath, in the hopes of minimizing the breakdown of milk protein (Carroll 2002, 14).

Homogenization heats and pressure-treats the milk to break up butterfat so that it distributes evenly, changing the molecular makeup of the milk. If you are 40-ish, like me, you might have heard your parents talking about the milk when they were young arriving with a cream top, where much of the fat separates into a thick, delicious layer at the top of the milk. My grandpa Louis skimmed this off for his coffee. I heard about cream-top milk growing up but did not experience it until I moved back to Colorado and found that a local dairy was offering milk that was pasteurized but unhomogenized. Check with your local dairy and see what they offer.

A small amount of milk that is out there on the shelf is ultrapasteurized or has undergone ultra-high temperature processing (UHT), where it is subjected to extreme heat to further shelf-stabilize it. Ultrapasteurized milk is heated to 191°F (88°C) for at least a second, creating a milk that will last at least 28 days refrigerated and unopened. Somewhat counterintuitively, most organic milk undergoes this extreme, high-heat processing to lengthen shelf life because it does not sell as quickly. UHT milk is heated to an even higher level than in ultrapasteurization. Both treatments damage proteins and destroy enzymes, so these products are unsuitable for cheesemaking.

RECIPES

The recipes collected here are a good entry point into cheesemaking and other dairy ferments. Direct acidification is an easy place to start, being a very approachable method for producing mild, rustic cheeses. From there, soft cheeses and other fermented dairy products offer a delicious gateway into the use of cultures. These recipes are generally scaled to use one US gallon (3.8 L) of milk. If you are feeling good about how things are coming out, you can scale up to two or three gallons, and from there up to five gallons (assuming you are giving away lots of cheese to friends and family).

The simple cheeses in this chapter require minimal equipment, but a good fine-mesh cheesecloth or butter muslin, a couple of plastic molds, and followers (whether fitted pieces of plastic, glass jars, or other nonreactive material sized to fit just inside the mold) to help form and shape the cheeses will take you a long way. Beyond those things are some regular kitchenware: a colander, a one-gallon or larger (say, 4 L and up) stainless steel or enameled pot, a thermometer, measuring spoons and cups, a strainer and ladle, and a long knife or other flat tool such as a long frosting spatula to cut the curds.

Karlin offers a good piece of advice for aspiring cheesemakers: know what you are trying to make. Track down some cheese in the style you are trying to replicate and eat it. Take photos of it to compare to your cheese. Familiarizing yourself with what your desired cheese looks, smells, and tastes like gives you an all-important frame of reference before you jump into creating it yourself (Karlin 2011, 6).

While cheesemaking book authors and commercial cheesemakers will urge you to maintain a pristine, sanitary environment, I personally go only as far as to maintain cleanliness. As with many other fermentations, there are myriad bacteria and wild yeasts that surround us, but a good standard of general cleanliness with your equipment and environment should prevent any massive contamination and allow a healthy cheese culture to crowd out any competition. Wash your equipment, wash your hands.

Herbs and Spices

A wide variety of ingredients can be added to your cheeses. Garlic, citrus zests, peppercorns, chile peppers, and herbs can be used to delicious effect. More delicate herbs, such as dill, basil, chives, and cilantro, should be used fresh. The flavor and aroma compounds that define these herbs are water-based, so as the herbs are dried, the flavor and aroma are carried off. In hardier, low-moisture herbs such as oregano and thyme, the flavor and aroma molecules do not dissipate as quickly so they can be used dried. If using pungent vegetables such as peppers or garlic, they should be chopped finely.

LEMON CHEESE

Contrary to its name, this is a very mild cheese with low acidity. Depending on how long the curds are allowed to set and how long it is allowed to drain, the cheese may be dry and crumbly or soft and creamy. Dry and crumbly works well with dishes such as lasagna or to sprinkle on soft tacos, but if you prefer a creamier texture then a splash of milk or cream can be mixed back into a dry batch of lemon cheese.

Lemon Cheese

Ingredients
- 3.8 L (1 US gal.) milk
- 125 mL lemon juice
  (the juice of 7–8 lemons)
- Kosher salt or cheese salt

Directions
1. Bring milk up to 190°F (88°C) degrees. Add lemon juice and mix thoroughly with an up-and-down motion for 15 seconds to fully incorporate.
2. When the curds give a clean break (typically after about 20 minutes), ladle them into a colander lined with fine-mesh cheesecloth. Tie the corners of the cheesecloth together and hang the cheese to drain for about an hour and a half, until no more whey is coming off the cheese.
3. Put the cheese into a bowl and mix in 10 g of salt, or to taste. Add back a splash of cream if a wetter, richer consistency is desired.

PANEER

Paneer is a great simple cheese to make. Very mild and great at absorbing flavors, it is the namesake cheese in the Indian dish *saag paneer*, a delicious mix of greens, paneer, spices, and coconut milk stewed together.

Paneer

Ingredients
- 3.8 L (1 US gal.) whole milk
- ¼ tsp calcium chloride
- 125 mL lemon juice

Directions
1. Add calcium chloride (see p. 83) to the milk and bring milk to a boil, stirring constantly to prevent scorching. When milk begins to foam up, turn off heat, continue stirring, and add lemon juice in a steady stream. Stir until you see a clean break between large curds and clear whey.
2. Let sit for 10 minutes and then ladle curds into a cheesecloth-lined colander. Give the curds a quick spray of cool water, just a couple of seconds, then allow to drain a few minutes.
3. Collect the corners of the cheesecloth and place in a mold on a draining mat. Weight with a quart or liter of water for 3–4 hours.

Paneer

© Getty/liubomirt

GREEK YOGURT

Yogurt is a food native to southeast Europe, Turkey, and the Middle East. According to some sources, it is the most popular fermented milk in the world (McGee 2004, 186). This recipe is for a thicker, Greek-style yogurt. Heating the milk beyond pasteurization before culturing leads to a thicker consistency by altering the casein protein.

Greek Yogurt

Note that this recipe only calls for a quart (0.95 L) of milk. While you can go larger, and the little sealed packet of yogurt culture can certainly inoculate more milk, you have to ask yourself what will you do with a gallon of yogurt. So, I have scaled this one back, but you are welcome to scale it back up and still use the following directions. (You could, for example, use the extra yogurt to make *labneh*, which is the next recipe.)

Ingredients

- ○ 0.95 L (1 qt.) milk
- ○ 1 packet yogurt culture, or 30 mL (⅛ cup) fresh yogurt from a recent batch

Directions

1. Very gently, bring the milk up to 200°F (93°C). Let cool to 110°F (43°C). Remove the skin on top of the milk.
2. Whisk in the yogurt culture using an up-and-down motion for 15 seconds to fully incorporate.
3. Hold the inoculated milk for 10 hours at 110°F (43°C). The simplest way to do this is with a programmable multicooker—for instance, an Instant Pot, which even has a yogurt setting. Another kitchen gadget option is to use a hot-water bath with an immersion circulator (sous vide). You can also put the pot of milk into a cooler filled with jars of hot water or use a heating pad for reptile cages (the heating pad could even be hooked up to a temperature controller).
4. Ladle the resulting yogurt into a container and refrigerate. It will thicken up as it cools.

LABNEH

A continuation of the previous recipe, *labneh* is also referred to as yogurt cheese. When you finish making a fresh batch of yogurt (see recipe left), there may be some residual whey that has separated out. To make labneh, put the yogurt you have just finished making into a cheesecloth-lined colander and allow to drain. This will give you a wonderfully thick, creamy spread that surpasses cream cheese and is great mixed with herbs and garlic and used for cooking. (Try stuffing boneless chicken thighs with labneh and roasting them.)

It is also a good reason to disregard the previous note on yogurt batch size; go ahead and double the milk for that recipe and set aside half of your yogurt for labneh.

Labneh

To make labneh, simply ladle a portion of your freshly made yogurt into a cheesecloth-lined strainer or colander and allow to drain for a few hours. When it has mostly stopped dripping, move it into a container and refrigerate. Like yogurt, the labneh will get thicker as it cools.

Labneh

© Getty/AlexPro9500

CHEVRE

This delicious, versatile goat's cheese is some really low-hanging fruit to get you into cheese-making. Do not get held up if you cannot find goat's milk, just make the adjustments and you will still be happy with it.

The chevre cultures on the market in America are direct-set mixes of bacteria and coagulant calibrated for one gallon (3.8 L) of milk, and the long rests at different stages make it easy to squeeze this into a busy schedule. I like to bring the milk up to temperature around 9:00 a.m. or 10:00 a.m., let it sit all day, and hang it to strain before bed. I let it hang overnight, then salt and form it in the morning.

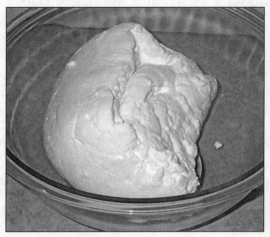

Chevre, shown here after hanging to drain, is a soft goat's cheese that is both delicious and easy to make.

Chevre

Ingredients

- 3.8 L (1 US gal.) whole goat's milk or cow's milk (If using pasteurized and homogenized cow's milk, add ¼ tsp calcium chloride and ⅛ tsp lipase.)
- 1 packet direct-set chevre culture
- zest of 1 lemon (optional)
- 1 tsp dried herbs such as thyme, rosemary, or herbs de Provence (all optional)

Directions

1. Gently warm milk to 85°F (29°C). Sprinkle the direct-set culture over milk and let sit for five minutes to hydrate. Whisk in the culture using an up-and-down motion for 15 seconds. Let rest for 12 hours.

2. After 12 hours, you should have a mass of coagulated curds separated from the whey. Using a slotted spoon, carefully ladle the curds into a cheesecloth-lined colander. Allow to drain for a few minutes, then tie the corners of the cheesecloth together and hang to drain into a bowl for about 8 hours. (If you find that you drained too long and have a drier, firmer chevre than you want, you can mix a couple of tablespoons of whey or cream back into the cheese.)

3. Add about ½–¾ teaspoon of fine sea salt per pound of cheese yield (1–1½ tsp per kilogram), plus optional lemon zest and herbs.

4. *Optional:* Pack cheese into cylindrical chevre molds or shape into the traditional log form by wrapping it in plastic wrap and rolling it into a cylindrical shape.

Chevre

Using Whey

If you are making your own cheese, there is a good chance that you maintain a certain "waste not" mindset and want to do something with your leftover whey, which makes up most of the milk you have bought or worked for. This byproduct of cheesemaking is full of protein, calcium, and other essential vitamins.

Many people who ferment at home will add whey to their sourdough starter or brined vegetables. While cheese cultures contain different strains of lactic-acid bacteria that will not necessarily kick-start your other fermentations, as is sometimes believed, the whey will lend subtle flavor and acidity to your bread doughs. Whey is also an excellent way to augment the stock you are using for soups and stews, and is a great base for a marinade, especially for pork.

It is even possible to double-dip, making two cheeses with the same milk. The separation of curds and whey in cheesemaking is not a 100% efficient method. In addition to casein, milk contains about half a percent of water-soluble albuminous protein, which does not come out of the whey during regular cheesemaking. It is possible to separate this protein, as well as the milk sugar, from the whey by cooking it to a much higher temperature.

Ricotta cheese, literally "recooked," can be made with whey from cultured cheese. The whey should be used as fresh as possible. To make traditional whey ricotta, gently bring the temperature of the whey up to 190°F (88°C). Remove from heat and add ½ teaspoon of salt, stirring to dissolve, followed by ¼ cup of vinegar per gallon of whey (16 mL per liter). Allow the whey and ricotta curds to sit for 15 minutes, then strain off curds into a colander lined with cheesecloth.

Two gallons of whey will produce up to a cup of ricotta (roughly 30 g ricotta for every liter of whey). To increase your yield, some of the whey can be replaced with skim milk, and a splash of cream can be stirred in to enrich the resulting ricotta cheese.

Feta

The classic Greek cheese, feta is great crumbled on salads, tossed with roasted vegetables, cubed for an antipasto plate, or generally used anywhere a firm, salty cheese is handy. This recipe is not as salty as many commercial versions; for a stronger flavor the salt level can be bumped up by 20%.

Feta

Ingredients

- ○ 3.8 L (1 US gal.) whole cow's milk or goat's milk (If using cow's milk, add ⅛ tsp lipase.)
- ○ ¼ tsp calcium chloride
- ○ ¼ tsp MA11 culture
- ○ ½ tsp liquid rennet, or ½ rennet tablet
- ○ Kosher salt or cheese salt

Directions

1. Gently heat the milk to 80°F (27°C). Add calcium chloride and stir to dissolve. Add culture and let sit for five minutes to hydrate.
2. After five minutes, stir the culture into the milk using an up-and-down motion to fully incorporate. Let rest 60 minutes.
3. After 60-minute rest, add ½ tsp rennet diluted in ¼ cup of unchlorinated water. Mix in the rennet using an up-and-down motion, then let rest another 60 minutes.
4. Cut curds into ½" pieces (1–1.5 cm), then let sit for ten minutes. Slowly raise the temperature to 90°F (32°C), stirring gently.
5. Continue stirring periodically for another ten minutes to prevent matting. Let rest for another ten minutes; the curds will sink to the bottom of the pot.
6. Ladle curds into a cheese mold placed on a draining mat. Put a follower on top of the mold, with a couple of cans of food or a quart/liter jar filled with warm water on top of the follower to press the cheese. Flip every two hours for six hours (i.e., three turns), then let sit under pressure overnight.
7. Cut wheel horizontally to give you two shorter rounds of cheese (roughly 1" or 2.5 cm tall). Salt each wheel with one tablespoon of kosher or cheese salt and let sit on a covered rack in a refrigerator. After 5–7 days, remove cheeses and wrap.

FROMAGE BLANC

Fromage Blanc

Ingredients
- 3.8 L (1 US gal.) whole cow's milk
- ¼ tsp MA11 cheese culture
- 4 drops liquid rennet
- ¼ tsp calcium chloride
- Kosher salt or cheese salt

Directions
1. Gently heat the milk to 75°F (24°C). Stir in calcium chloride and sprinkle the cheese culture on top of the milk. Allow culture to hydrate for five minutes, then stir it in using an up-and-down motion. Dilute the rennet in 60 mL (¼ cup) of unchlorinated water and add, using the same stirring motion to distribute. Let sit for 12 hours. (The temperature of your milk may drop into the high 60s Fahrenheit, or 19–20°C, while sitting; this is not a big deal.)
2. After 12 hours, you should have a mass of coagulated curds separated from the whey. Using a slotted spoon, carefully ladle the curds into a cheesecloth-lined colander. Allow to drain for a few minutes, then tie the corners of the cheesecloth together and hang to drain into a bowl for 6–8 hours.
3. Transfer cheese to a container and weigh it. Mix in about 2% salt by weight, or to taste. Refrigerate.

QUESO FRESCO

This queso fresco is a great mild cheese that melts well, and takes well to additions of chiles or herbs. I like it with jalapenos.

Queso fresco is a mild, easy-melting cheese that easily takes on additional flavors such as peppers and herbs.

Queso Fresco

Ingredients
- 3.8 L (1 US gal.) whole cow's milk
- ¼ tsp calcium chloride
- ¼ tsp MA11 cheese culture
- ¼ tsp liquid rennet, or ¼ rennet tablet
- Kosher salt or cheese salt
- 2–4 jalapeños, minced (optional)

Directions
1. Gently heat milk to 90°F (32°C). Add calcium chloride and stir to dissolve. Add cheese culture and let sit for five minutes to hydrate.
2. After five minutes, stir the culture into the milk using an up-and-down motion to fully incorporate. Let rest 60 minutes.
3. After the 60-minute rest, add the rennet diluted in 60 mL (¼ cup) of unchlorinated water. Mix in the rennet using an up-and-down motion, then let rest another 60 minutes.
4. Cut the curds into ½" (1–1.5 cm) pieces and let sit for 10 minutes. Slowly raise the temperature to 95°F (35°C) degrees over about 60 minutes while stirring regularly.
5. Ladle the curds into a cheesecloth-lined colander. Allow to drain for 15 minutes, then mix in 12 g salt and the jalapenos or other additions. (Some of the salt will be carried off with the whey as the cheese continues to drain.)
6. Transfer cheesecloth and curds to a round cheese mold on a draining mat. Put a follower on top of the mold, with 10 lb. (4.5 kg) of weight on top of the follower to press the cheese. Flip cheese every hour for 3 hours, then let sit for 6 hours or overnight under the weight. Remove cheese from the mold and refrigerate.

COTTAGE CHEESE

Cottage Cheese

Ingredients
- ○ 3.8 L (1 US gal.) skim milk
- ○ ¼ tsp MA11 cheese culture
- ○ ¼ tsp calcium chloride
- ○ Kosher salt or cheese salt

Directions
1. Gently bring milk to 72°F (22°C). Stir in the calcium chloride and sprinkle the cheese culture on top of the milk. Allow culture to hydrate for five minutes, then stir it in using an up-and-down motion. Let sit for 24 hours. (The temperature of your milk may drop into the high 60s Fahrenheit, or 19–20°C, while sitting; this is not a big deal.)
2. After 24 hours, you should have a clean break. Cut the curds and let sit for 15 minutes, stirring every five minutes. Heat the curds and whey very slowly to 110°F (43°C) over 45–60 minutes, stirring every five minutes. Let the curds rest at 110°F (43°C) for an hour, stirring every 10–15 minutes to keep from matting.
3. After an hour, strain off the curds into a cheesecloth-lined colander. Collect the corners of the cheesecloth together and pick up the cottage cheese bundle; rinse it with cold water for a minute to cool it and reduce the level of acidity. Allow to drain for five or ten minutes, then transfer to a container and weigh the cheese.
4. Add 1%–2% salt by weight, according to your preference. (You should yield around 1.6 lb. or 750 g of cheese, so salting will be about 7.5 to 15 g.) Stir to distribute salt and break up curds that have matted together.

CHEESE CURDS

A delicacy of the upper Midwest, especially Wisconsin and Minnesota, and in Canada, where they are piled on top of fries with gravy for poutine, fresh cheese curds are known for being squeaky, but they lose that property after aging for even a day. This is a great way to get them at their best, whether as a stand-alone snack or a topping. I like to dust them with some New Mexican red chile powder.

Cheese Curds

Ingredients
- ○ 3.8 L (1 US gal.) whole cow's milk or goat's milk (If using cow's milk, add ⅛ tsp lipase.)
- ○ ¼ tsp calcium chloride
- ○ ¼ tsp MA11 cheese culture
- ○ ¼ tsp liquid rennet, or ¼ rennet tablet
- ○ Kosher salt or cheese salt
- ○ red chile powder, cocoa powder, or dried herbs (all optional)

Directions
1. Gently heat the milk to 90°F (32°C). Add calcium chloride and stir to dissolve. Add the cheese culture and let sit for five minutes to hydrate.
2. After five minutes, stir the culture into the milk using an up-and-down motion to fully incorporate. Let rest 60 minutes.
3. After the 60-minute rest, add the rennet diluted in 60 mL (¼ cup) of unchlorinated water. Mix in the rennet using an up-and-down motion, then let rest another 60 minutes.
4. Cut curds into ½" (1–1.5 cm) pieces and let sit for ten minutes. Slowly raise the temperature to 100°F (38°C) degrees over about 30 minutes, stirring gently. Let rest at 100°F (38°C) for another 45 minutes. Continue stirring periodically to prevent matting.

5. Ladle curds into a cheese mold placed on a draining mat. Put a follower on top of the mold, with a couple of cans of food or a quart/liter jar filled with warm water on top of the follower to press the cheese.

6. Flip the cheese every 20 minutes for 3 hours. Cut into curds about ½"–1" by 1½"–2" (roughly 2 × 4 cm). Toss curds with 8 g of salt (about one tablespoon of coarse kosher salt) and let sit for ten minutes. Drain off any additional whey that has been expelled (the salt will draw moisture out of the curds) and taste; add a little more salt if necessary and toss with red chile powder, cocoa powder, or herbs, if desired.

Cottage Cheese

© Getty/oykuozgu

7

VINEGAR

Vinegar's history is inextricably tied to the history of alcohol. The word is a literal translation of the French *vin aigre*—"sour wine"—and vinegar would have been discovered hand-in-hand when humans began to produce wine some 6,000 years ago. As Harold McGee puts it, "Vinegar is alcohol's fate, the natural sequence to an alcoholic fermentation" (2004, 771).

In an aerobic environment, alcohol will inevitably be transformed into vinegar. Acetic acid, the fundamental component of vinegar, is produced primarily by acetic-acid bacteria of the genus *Acetobacter*, though *Gluconobacter* species can also follow the same metabolic pathway, that is, converting alcohol and oxygen into acetic acid and water. *Acetobacter* are hardy microbes that can survive moderate exposure to alcohol, which means that acetic acid has been one of humankind's most effective preservatives through the ages (McGee 2004, 771). Acetic acid can be effective at inhibiting microbial growth at levels as low as 0.1% of a solution. It is also an efficient fermentation, with the complete conversion of a 5% ABV solution resulting in a 4% acetic acid solution (and no ethanol). By comparison, fermentation by *Saccharomyces cerevisiae* only converts about 50% of a sugar solution into ethanol; the remainder is effectively lost as carbon dioxide. In an industrial setting, vinegar fermentation can be completed in a day. Modern vinegar is generally produced by trickling an alcoholic solution—this can be beer, wine, cider, or a mixture of pure distilled ethanol and water for white vinegar—over an air-rich matrix or by bubbling oxygen through the solution to promote rapid fermentation. The *Acetobacter* will metabolize acetic acid into water and carbon dioxide once it runs out of alcohol for fuel. After acetic fermentation is complete, the resulting vinegar is often aged for a few months to mellow and then pasteurized to kill off the *Acetobacter*.

Almost any solution with sugar can be fermented into alcohol, which can then be converted into vinegar. While Europeans were producing wine and aiming to drink it before it went bad (by turning into vinegar), the Chinese were harnessing the process to develop complex, grain-based vinegars. These products, which include the modern-day Chinese black vinegar, use some combination of rice, sorghum, wheat, barley, millet, and other ingredients, sometimes with roasted grains playing a role in the flavor profile.

At Noma, chef Rene Redzepi and his staff have learned how to make vinegar out of juices with little or no sugar, creating ingredients like fennel vinegar. His method is to add a small amount of neutral spirit (vodka or Everclear) to the juice of low-sugar fruits or vegetables and bubbling air through it with an aquarium pump for a couple of weeks. Spirits can even be used to produce gin vinegar, whiskey vinegar, or anything else that comes to mind. However, it is important to dilute the alcohol, whether with juice or water, when using a pure spirit for vinegar so that the acetic-acid bacteria can ferment it. A solution at 40% ABV, or even 15% ABV, is a very unwelcoming environment for even the most vigorous bacterial cultures. There is no hard and fast upper limit to the ABV for a vinegar fermentation, but above 10% to 12% will be increasingly stressful for *Acetobacter*, and will also give you an increasingly high, potentially unpleasant, level of acidity.

You can also take a cue from tradition and store your vinegar in barrels for a unique touch of flavor. Many small craft distillers are using small (5–15 gallon, or 19–57 L) barrels. You may be able to source one from your neighborhood distillery that was used for whiskey or other spirits. There are even smaller barrels, in the order of a few liters or less, available for the home bartender to barrel age a batch of cocktails. You can blend up a couple of liters of your favorite cocktail to age in one of these, then infuse your favorite vinegar with the residual character left in the barrel.

Literature on vinegar styles other than balsamic vinegar is sparse, probably because vinegar was always a natural byproduct tied to other existing products and rarely the result of intent. In balsamic vinegar production, the pinnacle of traditional methods, barrels play a key role in the process of fermentation and aging. It is important to note the difference between the watery red juice on your grocery store shelf labeled as balsamic vinegar, which is wine vinegar that may or may not be produced in Italy and have color and flavor added, and the rich, rare product labeled *Aceto Balsamico Tradizionale di Modena*.

Traditional balsamic vinegar, which is a protected designation of origin (abbreviated DOP in Italian) product, requires a minimum of 12 years of aging through a series of wooden barrels, resulting in a thick, syrupy vinegar that is intense and complex. It does not begin as wine, but as a cooked, concentrated grape juice called *mosto cotto*, which is made from the must of white, high-acid Trebbiano grapes and cooked down by about half.

Paul Bertolli, in his book *Cooking by Hand*, speaks reverently of the production of traditional balsamic vinegar, and discusses his process for producing balsamic-inspired vinegar in California. Because of the high sugar levels in the mosto cotto, Bertolli uniquely uses a *Zygosaccharomyces* yeast for the initial fermentation, which takes six to eight months:

> *A favorable peculiarity of this yeast is that its fermentation slows to a near standstill once it has produced alcohol in the range of nine percent, leaving the greater portion of its sugars intact. It is as though it knew to prepare the way for acetobacteria that thrive in moderately alcoholic liquids.* (Bertolli 2003, 72)

Once the *Zygosaccharomyces* fermentation has finished, it goes into large barrels and is inoculated with *Acetobacter*. After the vinegar has developed an optimal level of acidity, it then begins maturation.

Barrels for aging balsamic vinegar are made in ten different sizes, from 75 liters down to 10 liters (roughly 20 down to 2.5 gallons), and are tempered with a dry red wine and vinegar culture before being used for balsamic. A collection of casks for aging vinegar, known as a battery, can consist of three to ten barrels, all of different woods. Once the vinegar has fermented and acidified, it goes into the largest barrel to age, then is gradually transferred to progressively smaller and smaller casks, reducing in volume, thickening, and intensifying.

There is no strict rule for the order in which the different woods are used. That said, the softer, more porous woods that admit more oxygen in and let more water evaporate out are typically used for the larger-volume barrels. "The hardest woods with the most compact grain, such as oak and ash, are best suited to the smallest casks as they are more capable of holding old vinegar whose sugars have concentrated to heavy syrup" (Bertolli 2003, 67–68).

Every cask contributes its own character. For vinegar production, they are only filled 80% full, with a wider bung covered by a piece of cloth to let in oxygen. The battery is stored in the attic, exposing it to the full range of temperature fluctuations. In the winter, smaller casks are topped up from the immediately larger ones, with new mosto cotto made for the largest barrel.

In the first years, the aroma of the wood lays on top of the flavor of the vinegar. After four or five years, wood and vinegar begin to integrate as the vinegar's color darkens. After 10 to 15 years, the wood aromas recede and give way to a mellowing of the vinegar and a deepening of its perfume. In old age, the smell of the cask and the vinegar inside seem to be entirely joined to a singular bouquet with a complex underpinning. This merging of opposites, solid and liquid, happens by itself in its own good time. (Bertolli 2003, 68)

While 12 years is the threshold for DOP balsamico, there are other categories, including a three- to six-year *condimento balsamico*, and even a 25-year (or greater) Balsamico Extra Vecchio. Of all the fermented products, balsamic vinegar is something apart. "Balsamico is as much allowed to happen as it is made," states Bertolli,

Only a few things—wine, cured meat, and certain cheeses—improve with age. Even among these, balsamico stands apart in that it does not inevitably succumb to a descent in quality, the loss of a former

vitality, or the tragedy that follows ripeness. Rather, the older it grows, the higher it ascends. (Bertolli 2003, 74–75)

Chefs and cooks know the value of incorporating an acidic element into a dish to brighten and sharpen flavors, and to offset rich, heavy dishes. This elemental principle is evident in such far-flung dishes as English fish and chips with malt vinegar, Mexican street tacos with a squeeze of lime, and the tart tamarind notes in pad thai. Certain condiments make use of this principle. Yellow mustard, which is primarily composed of vinegar and turmeric, sets off the richness of hamburgers, hot dogs, and meaty sandwiches. Many commercial hot sauces rely on vinegar as much as on spice to make an impact.

Even drinks can be turned into something new and delicious with a touch of flavorful vinegar. Try a shot of raspberry or other fruit vinegar in a Pilsner, a gin and tonic, or some other light, easy-drinking, warm-weather drink of choice. A splash of acidity can enliven and enhance a wide range of dishes. Do not be shy about experimenting with it.

Author and cooking school founder Harry Rosenblum described his first experience making vinegar from a Brooklyn Brewery beer as a revelation. This approach eschewed the usual methods of most of the commercial malt vinegar varieties, which rely on a simple base of malted barley or corn and colored with caramel. Rosenblum found his malt vinegar was "complex, earthy, toasty, malty and tangy. It mimicked the flavors of the original brew—and was a perfect accompaniment for everything from seltzer to fries" (Rosenblum 2017, 11).

The FDA defines vinegar as having an acetic content of at least 4% (i.e., 4 g of acetic acid per 100 mL). White vinegar is often 5% acetic acid but contains no residual flavors or unfermentable sweetness to soften the acetic acid. A healthy vinegar fermentation with a starting ABV of above 5% should bring you within the FDA definition. Noma goes to 8% ABV, but anywhere from 5%–6% up to the low teens should be fine. One risk with starting higher than about 8% ABV is that it may make the vinegar too tart, but also *Acetobacter* can fail to ferment alcohol into vinegar once the ABV reaches 10% or more. The lower your ABV, the less acidic your finished vinegar will be, for better or worse. If you go with a higher starting ABV and find that your vinegar is too tart, you can add a splash of water to dilute it. For liquids with a high ABV to start, diluting with water prior to inoculation with *Acetobacter* is recommended for the best chance of success.

A basic vinegar, which starts with a moderate-strength alcoholic solution such as beer, wine, or cider, requires only more ingredient: a splash of unpasteurized vinegar. *Acetobacter*, like most of the other bacteria we rely on for fermentations, are everywhere, thriving wherever ethanol and oxygen are available. However, to ensure that nothing else takes hold and begins to grow in or on your would-be vinegar, it helps to make sure you start off with a plentiful, healthy culture by beginning with a mother of vinegar culture. These can be purchased online or at homebrew stores, or even obtained from a good quality unpasteurized commercial vinegar, such as Bragg's Cider Vinegar. Finding a gelatinous vinegar mother (similar to a kombucha SCOBY) is less important than using the freshest culture you can find. Buy your vinegar from a place that turns it over quickly; if the bottles are collecting dust, the bacterial culture may not be as vigorous as you need.

Acetobacter prefers to ferment at 75–100°F (24–38°C). Fermentation will be slow with lower temperatures, but room temperature is enough to keep a healthy *Acetobacter* culture chugging along. Use a wide-mouth, nonreactive container to allow for greater air flow. A growler or carboy might not allow enough oxygen to reach your vinegar, as compared to a glass jar or earthen crock. Be sure to keep your vinegar covered with a breathable material such as fine-mesh cheesecloth, a paper towel, or a coffee filter. While fruit flies are to be expected (and have even been identified as a transmission vector for acetobacteria), you probably do not want bugs flying around in your vessel and dying in your vinegar. When tasting your vinegar and assessing progress, remember that the acetic acid level will rise to an initial peak, then over additional months of aging will actually diminish slightly as the *Acetobacter* begins to digest acetic acid into

other compounds. It takes some of the edge off of a young batch of vinegar and leads to the development of additional flavors that will elevate your vinegar. Once finished, vinegar will keep indefinitely.

Rosenblum recommends two months to ferment, and you can begin to check your progress at three to four weeks. Keep an eye on your vinegar and make sure there is no mold that has developed on the surface. If mold does develop early on, before the pH drops, it can be skimmed off if caught quickly. Mold that develops later in fermentation is an indication that your ethanol is not converting into acetic acid, which should keep other microbial growth at bay.

Vinegar eels, harmless but off-putting, are another possible presence in your vinegar. Tiny worm-like nematodes, vinegar eels can be filtered out of your vinegar if you find an infestation. Kahm yeast can grow on fermenting vinegar before the pH drops far enough, but this will have minimal impact on the flavor of your vinegar.

You may also see a vinegar mother develop on top of your homemade vinegar. This is a cellulose mat created by the *Acetobacter*, similar to the phenomenon commonly seen in kombucha. The mother is not required for vinegar fermentation, so do not sweat it if one does not develop, it is not an indicator of quality.

Beer is an ideal medium for vinegar fermentation, but the antimicrobial properties of hops tilt the field toward choosing malt-forward beers that are full of character—porters, brown ales, stouts, English-style (i.e., more malty, less hoppy) barleywines. Smoke, black pepper, and chiles are natural accompaniments, whether in the original beer or infused in the beer during the vinegar fermentation. Try mixing the finished vinegar with a little brown sugar and red chile powder and cooking it down to make a glaze for ribs.

Other popular liquids include red wine, mead, and cider for more robust vinegars, and white wine or sake for more subtle vinegars. White wine or champagne vinegar are great bases for the addition of herbs, while the bright floral notes of some high-quality sakes can be an excellent foundation for high-quality rice wine vinegar. While distilled white vinegar will have a pH of 2.0 to 2.5, the less-pure vinegars here (adulterated as they are with flavorful ingredients) will finish closer to pH 3.0.

For a base liquid with an ABV above your desired level, such as a spirit or fortified wine, it can be diluted or some of the ethanol can be cooked off. Cooking off the alcohol is a less accurate method, but it is simple enough to pour the solution into a pot and bring it to a boil. You will notice the strong aroma of alcohol once the ethanol starts to evaporate off. Pull cooled samples regularly and taste; stop cooking when the base tastes less "boozy."

To be more accurate, use a little math and dilute the solution down to your target ABV. You need to first calculate the total amount of alcohol in the volume of base you have, which you can do if you know the starting ABV. Then calculate the new volume needed to yield your preferred ABV:

$$\text{total alcohol} = \text{vol.}_{start} \times \text{ABV}_{start}$$

Then,

$$\text{vol.}_{new} = \text{total alcohol} / \text{ABV}_{preferred}$$

The amount you add to dilute is the difference between the new volume and what you started with:

$$\text{water addition} = \text{vol.}_{new} - \text{vol.}_{start}$$

Let us do an example. For 100 mL of a 20% ABV fortified wine or liqueur, calculate the total amount of alcohol, then calculate the volume at your preferred ABV, which we will say is 7%:

$$\begin{aligned} \text{total alcohol} &= 100 \text{ mL} \times 0.2 \\ &= 20 \text{ mL} \end{aligned}$$

$$\begin{aligned} \text{vol.}_{new} &= 20 \text{ mL} / 0.07 \\ &= 286 \text{ mL} \end{aligned}$$

$$\begin{aligned} \text{water addition} &= 286 \text{ mL} - 100 \text{ mL} \\ &= 186 \text{ mL} \end{aligned}$$

RECIPES

PORTER OR STOUT VINEGAR

Try this with any stout or porter. It does not have to be barrel aged, but that adds layers of complexity. I preferred the vinegar that came from a barrel-aged Baltic porter from Denver brewery Station 26.

Barrel-Aged Baltic Porter Vinegar

Ingredients
- 355 mL (12 fl. oz.) barrel-aged porter or stout
- unpasteurized apple cider vinegar with live bacteria, or a previous batch of homemade vinegar, or a purchased mother of vinegar

Rich, dark beers are a great medium for beer vinegar, and additional factors such as whiskey and barrel aging bring further layers of flavor.

Directions
1. Add beer to a wide-mouth pint (0.25 L) canning jar. Agitate the vinegar to bring settled sediment back into solution and pour a tablespoon or two into the beer. Cover with a coffee filter secured with a rubber band or with the rim from a two-piece metal lid.

2. Ferment at room temperature for at least a month to fully convert, and longer to allow it to develop additional complexity.

3. For a smokey, spicy variation, throw a couple of dried chipotle peppers into the beer at the beginning of your vinegar fermentation. You could even drop in a couple of roasted cocoa beans or a teaspoon of cacao nibs to add a layer of chocolate character.

Vinegar

RED WINE VINEGAR

I like this with more robust red wines, like Malbec, Syrah, or Cabernet Sauvignon. With such a simple recipe, this is an excellent example of the principle of using excellent ingredients. The better the wine you choose, the better your vinegar will be.

Red Wine Vinegar

Ingredients
- ◯ 355 mL (12 fl. oz.) full-bodied red wine
- ◯ apple cider vinegar with live bacteria, or a previous batch of homemade vinegar, or a purchased mother of vinegar

Directions
1. Add wine to a wide-mouth pint (0.25 L) canning jar. If necessary, dilute to 10% ABV or less before inoculating. Agitate the vinegar to bring settled sediment back into solution and pour a tablespoon or two into the wine. Cover with a coffee filter secured with a rubber band or the rim from a two-piece metal lid.
2. Ferment at room temperature for at least a month to fully convert, and longer to allow it to develop additional complexity.

HERBED WHITE WINE VINEGAR

Naturally lighter in flavor than red wine, white wine is an excellent canvas to add flavors to. Start with a fruit-forward Chardonnay or an herbaceous Sauvignon Blanc and add some herbs fresh from the garden. This is a delicious vinegar to use in coleslaw or drizzled over roasted potatoes or vegetables.

White Wine Vinegar with Fresh Herbs

Ingredients
- ◯ 355 mL (12 fl. oz.) white wine
- ◯ 2–4 sprigs fresh herbs (thyme, rosemary, oregano, and tarragon are all excellent options), trimmed to fit your fermentation container
- ◯ apple cider vinegar with live culture, or a previous batch of homemade vinegar, or mother of vinegar

Directions
1. Add wine and herbs to a wide-mouth pint (0.25 L) canning jar, making sure that herbs are fully submerged. If necessary, dilute the wine to 10% ABV *after* the herbs have steeped. Agitate the vinegar to bring settled sediment back into solution and pour a tablespoon or two into the wine. Cover with a coffee filter secured with a rubber

White wine is a perfect base for fermenting into an herb-infused vinegar.

band or the rim from a two-piece metal lid.
2. Ferment at room temperature for at least a month to fully convert, and longer to allow it to develop additional complexity. Strain vinegar to separate any herb material.

RED VERMOUTH VINEGAR

Given the half-empty, dusty old bottle of cheap vermouth likely oxidizing away in the back of your liquor cabinet, it bears repeating that the better your ingredients, the better your final product will be. Splurge on a decent vermouth; it does not have to be a US$25 bottle, but it should be something you enjoy and would drink. Quality vermouth, traditionally infused with a variety of botanicals, is a complex and delicious product on its own. Fermenting it into vinegar replaces the sweetness with acidity, leaving you with a different but still excellent addition to cocktails. This recipe could also be adapted to other fortified wines and wine-based bitters in the range 18%–22% ABV.

Sweet/Red Vermouth Vinegar

Ingredients
- ○ 180 mL (6 fl. oz.) vermouth
- ○ 180 mL (6 fl. oz.) unchlorinated water
- ○ apple cider vinegar with live bacteria, or a previous batch of homemade vinegar, or mother of vinegar

Directions
1. Add wine and water to a wide-mouth pint (0.25 L) canning jar. Agitate the vinegar to bring settled sediment back into solution and pour a tablespoon or two into the wine. Cover with a coffee filter secured with a rubber band or the rim from a two-piece metal lid.
2. Ferment at room temperature for at least a month to fully convert, and longer to allow it to develop additional complexity.

PEAR VINEGAR

This is a great way to preserve that seasonal flavor you find at the farmers market, whether it is cherries, pears, blackberries, whatever. Swap out your preferred fruit by weight and proceed with the same directions.

A variety of fruits can be pureed and mixed with water and a sprinkle of yeast to create fruit vinegar.

Pear Vinegar

Ingredients
- ○ 1 large Comice or Asian pear (about 250 g)
- ○ apple cider vinegar with live bacteria or a previous batch of homemade vinegar
- ○ 50 g white sugar
- ○ sprinkle of champagne yeast (I prefer Lalvin EC1118)
- ○ white wine or unchlorinated water

Directions
1. Core the pear and puree in a blender or food processor. Transfer to a wide-mouth quart or liter canning jar. Agitate the vinegar to bring settled sediment back into solution and pour a tablespoon or two into the

fruit puree. Mix in sugar, a sprinkle of yeast, and enough wine or water to thin out the mixture (1–1½ cups, or 240–355 mL). Cover with a coffee filter secured with a rubber band or the rim from a two-piece metal lid.

2. Ferment at room temperature for at least a month to fully convert, and longer to allow it to develop additional complexity. Strain fruit pulp out and store.

GREEN CHILE AND PEACH VINEGAR

I prefer to pair green chiles from Pueblo, Colorado, which are meatier and fruitier than the more famous Hatch (New Mexico) green chiles, with fresh peaches from Colorado's Western Slope. Peach stands and chile roasters spring up all over the state when the harvest starts. Use the freshest peaches and chiles you can find, though, wherever they are from. This is delicious sprinkled over tacos instead of a lime wedge, or drizzled on grilled pork chops.

Peach-Chile Vinegar

Ingredients
- 2 medium peaches
- 2 roasted green chiles
- apple cider vinegar with live culture or a previous batch of homemade vinegar
- 50 g white sugar
- sprinkle of champagne yeast
- white wine or unchlorinated water

Directions
1. Pit the peaches. Remove the stems from the chiles (and, if desired, the seeds and ribs for reduced heat level), then puree the chiles and peaches in a blender or food processor. Transfer to a wide-mouth quart or liter canning jar.
2. Agitate the vinegar to bring settled sediment back into solution and pour a tablespoon or two into the fruit-chile puree. Mix in sugar, a sprinkle of yeast, and enough wine or water to thin out (1–1½ cups, or 240–355 mL). Cover with a coffee filter secured with a rubber band or the rim from a two-piece metal lid.
3. Ferment at room temperature for at least a month to fully convert, and longer to allow it to develop additional complexity. Strain pulp out and store.

8

KOMBUCHA

Kombucha is a particularly unique fermentation—a sweetened concoction, traditionally tea, transformed into an acidic, slightly funky drink by a slimy blob that floats on top. It is not the most instinctively appealing fermented product, but kombucha has exploded on the US market and in American kitchens over the last decade. Kombucha is part of a broader health and wellness trend that rolls up probiotics and gut health (super trendy buzzwords) together with a love of vaguely Far Eastern natural remedies (like turmeric). There are claims that it reduces your sugar intake by not drinking soda. However, if your kombucha tastes like some of the soda-like offerings off the shelf, then you are probably adding too much sugar, which is not great for your health and/or it means you are pulling it really early. So, let us talk about how to make good kombucha.

Commonly made using black tea, kombucha is the result of the actions of a symbiotic culture of bacteria and yeast (SCOBY for short), which includes a macroscopic part in the form of a gelatinous mat that floats on top and acts as an interface between the atmosphere and the tea. The SCOBY builds a raft of cellulose fibers, produced by the bacteria *Komagataeibacter xylinus* (formerly known as *Acetobacter xylinum*), with different microbes inhabiting different strata of the colony. This floating mat is actually a pellicle layer. Many kombucha makers will refer to this mat as the SCOBY, but technically the fermentative microbes are also in suspension in the liquid and not just hanging out in this mat. This mat is also called the "mother" (like in vinegar production), or the culture, the pancake, the tea fungus, even the mushroom. This pellicle formed by the culture protects the tea from invasion by other microbes, protects the anaerobic microbes that are part of the lower layers, and helps to reduce evaporation.

The primary activity of the SCOBY is a parallel fermentation by yeast and acetic acid-producing bacteria. The yeasts take up the sugar in the tea, converting it to CO_2 and ethanol. Meanwhile, the bacteria consume the ethanol and create acetic acid and water. It is the same combination of metabolic pathways used to make vinegar, but operating at the same time.

Where does kombucha come from? Who first found a questionable mass of goop on tea that had been sitting for weeks and said, "I'll give that a try!"? Nobody knows. The origins of kombucha are lost to history, but the oldest story dates it to China—also the original source of the tea plant—more than 2,200 years ago. However, tea was not regularly consumed until several hundred years or maybe even a thousand years later. Stories linking kombucha to ancient Korea or Japan likewise do not have a high level of credence or verifiability.

Any tea from the *Camellia sinensis* plant, whether black, green, white, oolong, or pu'erh, can be used for the base tea, though flavored teas (such as Earl Grey) might inhibit fermentation depending on the properties of the flavoring. The tea can be bagged or loose, weak or strong, but a good place to start is six to eight teabags or 6–8 teaspoons loose tea per gallon (3.8 L). Hannah Crum and Alex LaGory recommend a minimum of three tea bags per gallon to sustain the culture; more than 12 bags per gallon can begin to harm the SCOBY. Use unchlorinated water, whether boiled, filtered, spring, or distilled. Chlorine can interfere with microbiological activity; that is why it is in tap water, after all.

For those concerned about the caffeine content, it is worth considering that a normal-sized cup of tea is usually made with one bag. Tea for kombucha is a third to half as strong. There are studies that have shown the caffeine levels in kombucha decrease as it ferments, being reduced by as much as 33% within 24 hours and by 50%–65% after a week (Crum and Lagory 2016, 56).

Kombucha is a very old style of fermented tea with Asian origins that are lost to history.

For those wishing to lower the caffeine content further, the kombucha brewer can use a lower-caffeine tea such as green tea, or blend in herbal teas such as rooibos with regular tea. Some brewers of kombucha believe it is important to use at least 25% *Camellia sinensis* because rooibos and other herbal teas do not have fully oxidized tea leaves, which the SCOBY needs for nutrition to ferment the kombucha. Ideally, you would start with 100% *C. sinensis*, changing the percentage gradually with further batches to help your SCOBY acclimate. I have maintained a healthy kombucha culture for several generations with zero *C. sinensis*.

I would also caution the would-be kombucha brewer not to gamble their only SCOBY on an experimental batch. Because of the processing involved in decaffeinated teas, it is possible that residues from chemical treatment of the tea might inhibit proper fermentation. Standard decaffeinated tea is produced using a solvent called methylene chloride, and can contain a trace amount of this solvent below FDA limits. Organic decaffeinated tea may be produced using CO_2 extraction, so it is possible to find decaffeinated tea without residues that might interfere with your SCOBY.

Noma restaurant founder Rene Redzepi makes the point that "almost any liquid with enough sugar can be fermented into kombucha," and has made kombuchas from tisanes (herbal infusions) or fruit juices. These alternatives can "yield a roundness and depth of flavor not found in tea" (Redzepi and Zilber 2018, 110).

Redzepi has found that the tea flavor in kombuchas fades, and the consumer is "left with a one-note beverage that doesn't really take you on any sort of journey." Noma has experimented with all manner of solutions, including "off the beaten path" kombuchas that feature dairy, tree saps, and stocks made with chile peppers. "The kind of kombucha we're chasing bears very little resemblance to the sour liquid people force themselves to drink because it's supposedly good for them" (Redzepi and Zilber 2018, 111).

Just as the liquid medium can be varied, so can the sugar source. Pure white sugar is the standard workhorse, but evaporated cane juice can contain residual vitamins and minerals that benefit the SCOBY and the consumer, while darker sugars such as demerara or piloncillo, or even honey and maple syrup, can be used to add their own flavor notes to the kombucha (though the native bacteria in raw, unpasteurized honey can compete with the SCOBY and create unpleasant results).

A good baseline is to use about one cup of sugar per gallon (approx. 55 g per liter). You may want to use more or less; Crum and LaGory recommend as little as ½ cup and as much as two cups (approx. 25 to 105 g per liter). For the brewer or homebrewer with a hydrometer or refractometer, Noma recommends starting with 12°Brix for kombucha (12% sugar by weight; note the amounts mentioned above range from 2.6% to 10%). More sugar is more fuel for fermentation activity and will result in more ethanol, organic acids, flavor compounds, other fermentation byproducts, and levels of live culture in the tea. An elevated level of sugar will lead to a kombucha that is sweeter at first and more acidic later, and more strongly flavored overall in the middle stages. Crum and LaGory note that the sugar is reduced by 50%–70% between seven and 14 days, and up to 80% after 30 days.

To help keep the sweetened tea at a safe pH during the first few days of fermentation, 5%–10% of mature kombucha (or a couple tablespoons of vinegar if you have no kombucha on hand) needs to be added to every new batch. The kombucha will naturally fall into a safe zone in a few days, dropping to pH 3.5 within four or five days.

The final ingredient is the SCOBY. A SCOBY can vary in looks, color (white to light brown), and texture (smooth or bumpy). A daughter SCOBY will form on top of a new batch and can eventually be separated to be used or given away. A mother SCOBY can be purchased online from a large number of suppliers, including https://www.kombucha.de or GEM Cultures; or you might be able to find one at a local farmer's market or homebrew supply store near you, or online markets/communities such as Nextdoor or Craigslist. Also, any kombucha maker would be glad to share their starter tea and SCOBY with you. I have effectively used the method outlined in the *Art of Fermentation* (Katz 2012) to grow a SCOBY from a store-bought bottle of kombucha: pour the kombucha into a wide-mouth pint jar, cover it with a cloth or coffee filter, and wait two or three weeks until a new SCOBY forms.

This easy grow-your-own approach will appeal to the homebrewer who enjoys harvesting yeast cultures from their favorite exotic, bottle-fermented beers. The SCOBY you create with this method will probably have a smaller diameter than your half-gallon or gallon jar, but do not worry, a healthy SCOBY will grow to cover the surface of the tea in your larger kombucha jar. Do not be afraid of some trial and error. Different kombucha brands may have different processing methods, and grocery-store kombucha may have been on the shelf for months, giving you a stressed biological specimen. It may take some time to find a commercial example that works best for you.

Once you have your sweetened tea or other solution, the last key piece is a vessel. Glass is excellent, as is nonreactive plastic. As with pickling, high-quality stainless steel is usable, but lower-quality metals will be corroded by the acidity and leach into the tea. And in general, stainless steel is more expensive and does not allow you to see inside your vessel.

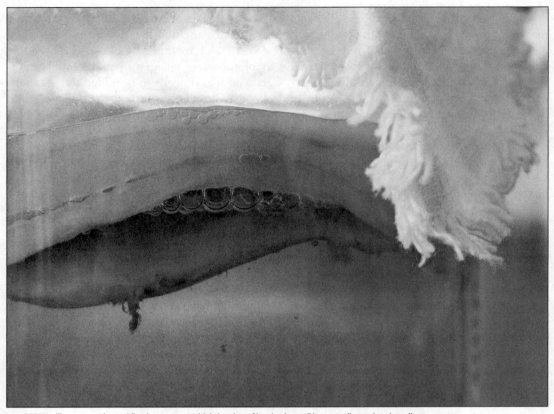

Your SCOBY will grow over time, adding layers over multiple batches of kombucha until it eventually needs to be split. © *Getty/Premyuda Yospim*

A jar with a plastic spout at the bottom is a convenient way to pour off tea without having to remove the SCOBY, but be sure to find a high-quality, hard plastic spigot with a commercial-grade gasket. Look out for glue, paint, or metallic finish that may erode and dissolve into the kombucha.

Once your would-be kombucha is brewed and combined with your SCOBY in the fermentation vessel, it needs to be covered with a light cloth, fine cheesecloth, coffee filter, or paper towel to keep out pests such as fruit flies (secure the covering with a rubber band). It is important that the SCOBY is able to take up oxygen; kombucha is both an aerobic and anaerobic fermentation, so the top layers need access to oxygen as the SCOBY interfaces between the air and the liquid medium. Once the cellulose mat forms, the acetic acid fermentation will proceed anaerobically. The original pellicle that was added will drop to the bottom as the daughter takes its place at the top of the fermenting kombucha.

Kombucha prefers to ferment out of direct sunlight at about 75–85°F (24–29°C). It should take about 10 days, but in a cool space below 70°F (21°C) it can take months to reach the desired state. As a result, you may find that your kombucha takes longer to attenuate in the winter. But do not worry, as long as the kombucha is being held in an environment of at least 65–66°F (~18°C), it will get there. Any cooler and the bacterial action will slow down too far and the kombucha will be off-balance and susceptible to infectious growth. Even in the winter, most homes have a space that maintains a temperature somewhere between 65°F and 70°F (18–21°C); check the top of your water heater or that inconvenient little cabinet up above your stove. Changes in temperature will result in different microbes being more active at certain times—this means the microbial makeup of a cooler fermentation will be different to that of a warmer fermentation, so there will be differences in flavor as well. The exact microbial composition of a kombucha will vary quite a bit as a result of environmental conditions.

There are also equipment options for keeping your kombucha warm. When I lived in the mountains and was learning to homebrew, I often needed to rely on a heated belt that went around my carboy during the winter. There are wraps available that are sized for carboys or smaller glass jugs, and heater mats that your fermentation vessel can be put on top of. If you want to be extra precise, the heater can be run through a temperature controller attached to a probe in the kombucha (assuming you are using a stainless steel probe that will not degrade in the acidic environment).

After a week, or sooner if you are fermenting above 80°F (27°C), start tasting your brew periodically (this is where a spigot comes in handy). The kombucha is ready when you are happy with it. It should have some residual sweetness and enough acidity to brighten it up. The "ideal" moment for kombucha is very subjective, and the balance will constantly shift as it continues to ferment.

Because it will continue to ferment, if you are looking for carbonation you should bottle your kombucha when it is still a little too sweet and leave it at room temperature for a few days before putting it in the refrigerator. Pulling the kombucha when the fermentation is "just right" to carbonate and maintain the desired flavor profile is very much a balancing act. Unlike with beer brewing, the kombucha brewer does not usually carbonate after the product has been fully attenuated. Priming sugar can be used the same way as in homebrewing, and kegging and force-carbonating is also effective. If a bottled kombucha is primed and left on the shelf for too long before refrigeration it can become overcarbonated and lead to foam-outs when opened, or even bursting bottles. Given the potential variability, I tend to pour off my kombucha into a growler and stash it in the fridge. After a few days, it will clarify and look much more appealing. If you are determined to carbonate, though, a SodaStream or similar countertop carbonator might be the easiest option. My wife found ours for $25 at a yard sale.

Along with using consistent levels of sugar and reliable fermentation conditions, a pH meter or pH strips can be used to help set benchmarks for when to pull kombucha, when to bottle it, and when to refrigerate it. I like my kombucha to reach a final pH of about 3.

More so than with other ferments, pulling kombucha and consuming or cooking with it at the right time is critical. At Noma, we often freeze our kombuchas to halt fermentation and ensure that they're held at the top of their curve. (Redzepi and Zilber, 2018, 115)

Kombucha can be flavored with fruit, vegetable juice, spices, and herbs. Fruit can be used fresh, dried, juiced, or pureed. Herbs can be dried or fresh, but more volatile herbs such as mint, basil, or cilantro should be used fresh and chopped. *The Big Book of Kombucha* (Crum and LaGory 2016) even calls for ingredients such as garlic, mushrooms, avocado, and bacon in some recipes. Flavoring can be added during fermentation for a more incorporated flavor that has undergone fermentation with the tea. Kombucha can also be flavored in the bottle or in a secondary container for a few days.

If you prefer bottles without cloudiness, chunks, or bits of flavoring in them, the kombucha can be transferred to a secondary container, flavored according to preference, then bottled. It can also be filtered at this time by pouring through cheesecloth, if desired. If using this secondary stage, you need to account for the extra time the brew will continue to acidify, so you should pull the kombucha when it is still sweeter than you would prefer. A secondary fermentation in a sealed jar will create anaerobic conditions, potentially short-circuiting the activity of acetic-acid bacteria and creating more alcohol and lactic acid than in an open-fermented vessel. Before bottling, you can filter the kombucha either physically using a coffee filter or chinois, or using an additive like bentonite, which is commonly used in winemaking.

As you monitor the progress of your kombucha, be wary of changes to your SCOBY that might indicate infection or an unhealthy culture. Redzepi and Zilber warn against colorful molds—pink, green, or black—on your SCOBY as an indication that the starting tea was not acidified enough to prevent potentially dangerous growth:

> *Pathogenic mold can produce harmful toxins that dissolve into the liquid. Trying to identify whether an invasive mold is malignant or benign isn't worth the risk. You can always brew more kombucha.*
> (Redzepi and Zilber 2018, 126)

However, your SCOBY is a sturdy culture. It can be left unattended for months without adverse effects; simply store it in the fridge or a cool place in some extra kombucha and give it a feeding of fresh tea when you are ready to use it again. It can also be fed at intervals, like with sourdough, discarding a cup or two and adding fresh sweetened tea to keep the culture healthy.

Kombucha brewers can use either a batch approach, building a batch and adding a SCOBY (with up to 10% by volume of mature kombucha) to ferment and bottle, or more of a solera-style method, where part of the kombucha is drawn off and the container is topped up with fresh tea. With a significant amount of kombucha "starter" remaining, fermentation can take much less time, in some cases only a few days to finish. Depending on how often and how dramatically you vary your kombucha recipe, this continuous method can produce a kombucha with more varied and complex flavors than a single batch. However, you need to think through the progression of flavors being added to your kombucha solera and not combine new flavors that clash with the existing batch.

The SCOBY, over time, will get thicker and thicker if you do not peel part of it off to give away or split off new batches. It will eventually need to be trimmed down, cutting it laterally to less than a half-inch thickness (<13 mm).

The Alcohol and Tobacco Tax and Trade Bureau (TTB), the federal agency that regulates alcohol manufacture and sales, requires that "nonalcoholic" beverages such as kombucha (as well as fruit juices, which can ferment slightly while on the shelf) clock in below 0.5% ABV. However, when the TTB tested several off-the-shelf sample kombuchas in 2010, they found a high proportion of violations, some being up to 3% ABV, leading to widespread product recalls and reformulations. In a subsequent round of testing in 2015, the TTB again issued fines and warning letters to commercial kombucha brewers about exceeding the legal alcohol limit.

Homebrewed kombucha can easily come in at 2%–3% ABV. Since kombucha is the result of multiple simultaneous fermentations, a complex mix of sugar, alcohol, water, and acid, all with different densities, there is no simple and accurate way to measure the ABV, Brix, or gravity at home. (You might try to befriend the lab manager at your local craft brewery and bribe them to run your juice through a gas chromatograph.) A lower sugar level and shorter fermentation will give you lower levels of both alcohol and organic acids.

Eventually, the final stage of a kombucha ferment is where it becomes vinegar, either when all the available sugar and alcohol has been consumed or the SCOBY reaches its pH tolerance. This takes several weeks up to a few months. Kombucha vinegar is less intense than commercial vinegar, possibly being around 2% acidity versus 4%–7% (Crum and LaGory 2016, 256). The tea and other flavoring ingredients will also impact the flavor profile of this end-state kombucha, potentially softening the impression of acetic acid. Kombucha vinegar can be used for salads, quick pickles, and other recipes in place of apple cider vinegar or red wine vinegar.

WELLNESS CLAIMS

Maybe more than any other fermented food, kombucha has been the subject of a dizzying array of health claims. (For more on the discussion of probiotics in fermented food, see "The Wellness Trend" in chapter 1.)

According to Sandor Katz (2012, 167), "Kombucha has inspired much polarized debate, with claims of dramatic curative properties matched by dire warnings of potential dangers. My own conclusion is that both sets of claims tend to be exaggerated." He goes on to list ailments that the drink has allegedly cured—"arthritis, asthma, bladder stones, bronchitis, cancers, chronic fatigue syndrome, constipation, diabetes, diarrhea, edema, gout, hay fever, heartburn, high blood pressure, high cholesterol, kidney problems, multiple sclerosis, psoriasis, prostate disorders, rheumatism, sleeping disorders, and stomach and bowel disorders"—but notes there is no scientific data to back up these claims (Katz 2012, 168). So, is kombucha just another snake oil in a long series of wellness fads?

Crum and LaGory (2016, 7) state that kombucha, rather than being a curative for specific ailments, "gives the body the opportunity to return to balance so that the immune and other physiological systems function more efficiently." To be fair, this is not exactly an unbiased piece of scientific research: my copy of the book states in large font on the back cover "Brew for Health." Nonetheless, kombucha is shown to contain a long list of amino acids, including many essential amino acids, as well as a variety of organic acids, antioxidants, and glucuronic acid, which is usually produced by the liver to bind up and remove toxins and waste products.

In the *Annals of Epidemiology*, Julie Kapp and Walton Sumner surveyed the existing research, and found one study out of 262 relating to kombucha that reported empirical results of kombucha on humans:

Our literature search identified no controlled studies of human subjects, only one study examining any health benefits of kombucha from human subjects research and no studies in the 15 years since [a previous literature review]. Nonetheless, significant commercial shelf space is now dedicated to kombucha products, and there is widespread belief that the products promote health. (Kapp and Sumner 2019, 68)

Kapp and Sumner did highlight that there is a wide-open opportunity for research regarding human health, including an examination of the relationship between the broader historical absence of traditional fermented foods—including kombucha—in the United States and "population health outcome trends" such as diabetes and obesity (2019, 69). Crum and LaGory note the same potential connections: "The more we understand the effects of diet and stress on our human organism, the more it becomes obvious why kombucha is of such great benefit for so many of our modern diseases" (Crum and LaGory 2016, 13).

RECIPES

You will see a general trend in my approach to kombucha flavorings. Citrus (lemon, lime, orange) or citrusy (coriander, lemongrass, lemon balm, lemon thyme) ingredients are a natural fit for the tart notes of kombucha. Except in the case of orange, which is less acidic, the citrus juice itself is too tart. Rather, the zest of these fruits makes an excellent flavor addition. Ginger is an excellent addition, along with all sorts of brightly flavored spices. Many other fruits or juices, such as cherry, raspberry, or pineapple, are also excellent pairings with the acidic, fruity notes in kombucha.

Fresh herbs (basil, mint, cilantro) are delicious, and on occasion I will go to heartier herbs such as thyme or rosemary. Many of these flavor combinations are arbitrary and can be mixed and matched as you like. I prefer simplicity. I like to work with a few ingredients that come together cohesively, but feel free to explore other avenues and flavor combinations. You may prefer a kitchen-sink approach to kombucha, throwing some herbs, a couple types of fruit, and some spices all into the same batch.

Because the tea (*Camellia sinensis*) in kombucha contributes nutrients that are important to the health of a SCOBY, you may find it wise when experimenting with non-standard solutions, such as juice or herbal teas, to use extra SCOBYs that grow as part of the regular kombucha-making process. Do not gamble with your sole healthy SCOBY to experiment with something adventurous like a cherry-cacao-chipotle kombucha, because you might find that your brilliant vision is actually a biological dead end. But do not be afraid to experiment, and have patience. I have put up two kombuchas on the same day with healthy SCOBYs. The one brewed with a fruit-based tea took two weeks longer to finish, but it was delicious and the SCOBY performed just fine on future batches.

BASIC KOMBUCHA

This is your entry-level, kombucha 101 recipe. It can easily be halved or quartered; I use a half-gallon batch size (roughly 2 L) to experiment with new flavor combinations. Or it can be doubled if you are going through that much kombucha.

Sweetened tea is the base medium for kombucha to ferment.

Basic Kombucha

Ingredients
- 6 bags black tea
  (or 6 tsp of loose-leaf black tea)
- 200 g (1 cup) white sugar
- 3.8 L (1 US gal.) unchlorinated water
- healthy SCOBY
- 150 mL (5 fl. oz.) mature kombucha or a big splash of cider vinegar

Directions
1. Bring water to a boil in a pot. Steep tea bags in the pot for five minutes then remove them. Add sugar and stir to dissolve. (Adding the sugar while the water is still warm will help it to dissolve.)

2. When your tea has reached room temperature, pour it into your kombucha jar, add your SCOBY and mature kombucha or vinegar, and cover with a breathable material (cheesecloth, kitchen towel, paper towel). Do not worry if your SCOBY sinks initially. It may eventually float to the top, or the cultures present in it will populate the tea and create a new SCOBY on top of your tea. If neither happens, your SCOBY is no longer viable.

3. Begin tasting your kombucha at one week. One way to do this is by using a clean straw, putting it into the kombucha (pushing aside the pellicle) and holding your finger over the end while lifting it out. This allows you to get a taste without disturbing the mat or the contents. At two weeks, you should be getting closer, but how quickly you arrive at "done" is a matter of fermentation temperature and personal preference.

For your first batch or two, it may be educational to pull off and refrigerate half of your batch for consumption and leave half to continue fermenting. Keep tasting until it is past where you want it, and then top up your fermentation jar with a half-batch of fresh kombucha, which will be ready even faster than the first round. Sometimes the best way to know how far to go is to go too far and then dial it back next time.

Variations
Using green tea. Add the zest of two limes and 80 g of ginger sliced ¼" (6 mm) thick in the initial fermentation. (The thinner you slice the ginger, the faster it will extract into the tea.) This method of fermenting with the added ingredients will create a kombucha with lime and ginger flavors that are more cohesively incorporated, rather than flavors layered on top of the fermentation. Splash an ounce or two (30–60 mL) into your favorite Pilsner for a unique take on a shandy.

You can swap in fresh lemon thyme for lime in green-tea kombucha. Add 16 sprigs of lemon thyme and 80 g of ginger sliced ¼" (6 mm) thick in the initial fermentation. Make sure that the lemon thyme is fully submerged, otherwise the exposed part of it will grow mold. Lemon thyme, while adding a distinctly citrusy note, will accentuate the savory, woody, earthy notes of the green tea and the ginger. This version makes a great whiskey highball.

Using black tea. When fermentation is close to completion, transfer the kombucha to another container. Add 340 g (12 oz.) of fresh raspberries and 7–8 sprigs of mint, making sure that the mint is submerged. (The raspberries will float on top.) After a week or less, your kombucha should be well-infused and ready to strain out.

Those are just a few of the limitless flavor variations available if you only use tea for the base. When you open the door to tisanes (herbal teas) and fruit juice, the options really go through the roof. You can try substituting them 100% for traditional tea, or try mixing and matching teas and herbal teas, like four bags of green tea and four bags of lemon ginger tea for a gallon (3.8 L) of kombucha.

You do not have to restrict yourself to bagged tea from the grocery store, either. There are a number of modern tea blenders making interesting, unique, loose-leaf teas that go beyond green and black tea, incorporating flavors of fruit, herbs, even nuts and chile peppers. Capri, a caffeine-free blend of dried melon and mint from August Uncommon Tea, is one of my favorite bases for kombucha. The fruit flavor is a perfect match for the tart fermentation character of kombucha. Another excellent option August offer, Big Easy, is a blend of green tea, lemongrass, pineapple, and barley. You may have a tea blender in your area, or a favorite tea company that you order from online. Reach out and see if they have some recommendations on where to start in their library, or if they can suggest herb/spice/fruit additions that would pair with specific teas and enhance your kombucha. There are other flavors out there that might not be as intuitive. Split off a small batch and experiment, then scale it up when you hit on something you love.

Kombucha

© Getty/Premyuda Yospim

PINEAPPLE-GREEN TEA KOMBUCHA

Pineapple and Green Tea Kombucha

Ingredients
- ○ 4 bags of green tea
- ○ 2.4 L (80 fl. oz.) unchlorinated water
- ○ 135 g (⅔ cup) sugar
- ○ 1.2 L (40 fl. oz.) pineapple juice
- ○ 150 mL (5 fl. oz.) mature kombucha or a big splash of cider vinegar
- ○ 2 tbsp ground coriander
- ○ 1½ tbsp pink peppercorns, crushed coarsely
- ○ healthy SCOBY

Directions
Brew tea and incorporate sugar. Once cooled, add pineapple juice, mature kombucha or vinegar, and spices. Transfer to fermentation vessel. Add SCOBY and ferment as desired.

LEMON BALM KOMBUCHA

Using lemon balm results in a delicious, citrusy, caffeine-free substitute for *Camellia sinensis*. If you have a garden, lemon balm is an easy-growing perennial related to mint.

Lemon Balm Kombucha

Ingredients
- ○ 3.8 L (1 US gal.) unchlorinated water
- ○ 200 g approx. (3–4 cups) loosely-packed lemon balm leaves
- ○ 200 g (1 cup) white sugar
- ○ healthy SCOBY
- ○ 150 mL (5 fl. oz.) mature kombucha or a big splash of cider vinegar

Directions
Bring water to a boil in a pot. Steep lemon balm leaves in the pot for five minutes then remove them. Add sugar and stir to dissolve. When your tea has reached room temperature, pour it into your kombucha jar, add your SCOBY and mature kombucha or vinegar. Ferment as desired.

BASIL / LEMONGRASS / STAR ANISE

Essentially a basil-lemongrass tea flavored with star anise, this is a classic combination of Asian flavors, especially if you can find or grow an anisey Thai variety of basil. The star anise is a subtle addition that softens the acidity of the kombucha.

A combination of basil, lemongrass, and star anise is a flavorful substitute for tea in kombucha.

Basil-Lemongrass Tea and Star Anise Kombucha

Ingredients
- 3.8 L (1 US gal.) unchlorinated water
- 150 g (5.3 oz.) basil
- 50 g (1.8 oz.) lemongrass, chopped
- 10 g (0.4 oz.) star anise pods
- 200 g (1 cup) sugar
- 150 mL (5 fl. oz.) mature kombucha or a big splash of cider vinegar
- healthy SCOBY

Directions
Bring water to a boil. Remove from heat and steep basil, lemongrass, and star anise for at least five minutes. Add sugar and stir to dissolve. When tea is cooled to room temperature, add mature kombucha or vinegar, transfer to fermentation vessel. Add SCOBY and ferment as desired.

CHERRY-VANILLA KOMBUCHA

This recipe does not need any added sugar, it all comes from the cherry juice.

Cherry and Vanilla Bean Kombucha

Ingredients
- 0.45–0.50 L (about 2 cups) cherry concentrate
- 10–15 vanilla beans (depending on size), split open half lengthwise
- 150 mL (5 fl. oz.) mature kombucha or a big splash of cider vinegar
- healthy SCOBY

Directions
Dilute the cherry concentrate to almost 3.8 L (1 US gal.) using unchlorinated water. Transfer to fermentation vessel, add vanilla beans, mature kombucha or vinegar, and SCOBY. Ferment as desired.

9

CHARCUTERIE

The twenty-first century has been kind to the field of charcuterie. Popular appreciation for preserved and prepared meats has exploded in recent decades. Twenty years ago, the selection in America was limited largely to mass-produced bacon, cold cuts (deli meats), and bratwurst or Italian sausages. Nowadays, regional specialties from around the world are stocked at upscale grocers, we have boutique local producers who use high-quality local meats and focus on unique flavors, and a charcuterie and cheese board is on the menu at every chic, meat-forward restaurant and brewpub.

The word itself—a French word that comes from the roots *chair* (meat) and *cuit* (cooked)—was once a sort of secret handshake among aficionados. If you knew what "charcuterie" was, you were on the inside track. You knew there was more out there. As Taylor Boetticher and Toponia Miller write, "At its most basic level, charcuterie is the technique of seasoning, processing, and preserving meat. But it is also a way of preserving food cultures and traditions, and enriching our daily habit of breaking bread" (Boetticher and Miller 2013, 2).

Charcuterie is a term that applies to a broad array of prepared or cured meats. Techniques include salting, grinding, smoking, drying, fermenting, and cooking. Different methods are applied to different muscle groups based on their composition, namely, the ratio of meat to fat and the type of fat.

Making charcuterie presents a unique set of challenges. Of all the fermentation media included in this book, animal flesh is the most prone to decay and its accompanying health risks. If you leave a cucumber on the counter it may not be in prime condition after a few days but it is still going to be edible. If you leave a pork chop on the counter for three or four days, it will result in an unmistakable aroma that permeates your home. Animal flesh is the least stable of any food we eat and will rapidly go off and putrefy at typical ambient temperatures. It is particularly susceptible to contamination by pathogenic bacteria and, thus, can be a potentially dangerous vector for food poisoning (Katz 2012, 337).

Nonetheless, cultures around the world have developed methods to preserve a seasonal or periodic bounty for future use. Often, these proteins were not the centerpiece in the meals that the average person ate, but touches that enlivened other foods—a piece of salt pork in a pot of beans, a touch of intensely funky fish sauce or fish paste in a bowl of noodles and vegetables, a piece of "corned" beef (named for the salt corns that preserved it) in a stew of vegetables and potatoes. The modern American meal, with a hearty chunk of meat in the middle of the plate, is, of course, a historical oddity.

Making shelf-stable meats is all about reducing water activity (a_w, *see* pp. 9–10) and creating an environment hostile to spoilage bacteria. Drying removes moisture; salting locks up moisture; and salt (NaCl), sodium nitrate ($NaNO_3$), sodium nitrite ($NaNO_2$), and acidity create an inhospitable environment for bacterial growth.

All three of these processes also help to concentrate or develop the flavor of a product and are used in various combinations, depending on the intended result. A summer sausage is dried a little (but less than a salami), has both salt and sodium nitrite, and is fermented to create lactic acid. Whole-muscle dry curing for products like ham or coppa (an Italian sausage) does not require acidification or sodium nitrite, because the interior flesh is sterile. (This is the core principle of dry-aged steaks, as well. A large cut of meat can be hung to age, with moisture loss and enzymatic reactions intensifying the flavor of the interior meat, while the exterior begins to rot. The outside can then be trimmed away and what remains can be a much more flavorful, if also much more expensive, version of the original cut.) However, sodium nitrite can also be used on whole muscles for the unique flavor and color the curing salt provides, as well as its ability to prevent fat from going rancid.

On Nitrates and Nitrites

The curing salts sodium nitrate ($NaNO_3$) and sodium nitrite ($NaNO_2$) have been the subject of a good deal of unfortunate reporting. Much like the fear that surrounded the use of another type of salt, monosodium glutamate, the widespread health concerns over the use of nitrates and nitrites have far outrun the science.

When curing meat under certain conditions, nitrates and nitrites are essential, as even the FDA concedes. However, when cooked under high heat, nitrites may convert into nitrosamines, which are carcinogenic. (In the body, nitrates can be converted in the body into nitric oxide, a signaling molecule that lowers blood pressure.)

Regarding the original study identifying nitrosamine production in cured meats, Steve Ettlinger writes in the book *Ingredients*, "Not only were facts and conditions elusive, the only thing scientists did seem to agree on at the time was that dangerous levels were found only in certain kinds of overcooked bacon" (Eschliman and Ettlinger 2015, 156) This scare continues to affect consumer choices today, as seen by the proliferation of "uncured" and "no nitrates added" meats. However, these products are in no way free of nitrates, they are simply marketing gibberish that takes advantage of a loophole in labeling laws. Spinach, lettuce, and radishes can contain almost 2,000 parts per million (ppm) of sodium nitrate, and producers of "uncured" products use these ingredients as their source of nitrates.

The USDA allows for up to 156 ppm of nitrite added to cured meat, "but typically, even at the common level of 120 ppm, only about 10 ppm remains after processing" (Eschliman and Ettlinger 2015, 156). This is because sodium nitrite in the meat reduces in an acidic environment to nitric oxide, which then reacts with myoglobin in red blood cells, stabilizing the red color in cured meat. Further, "vegetables are the source of up to 80 to 90 percent of our nitrite consumption," Ettlinger writes. When making "uncured" products, "Instead of adding the chemical directly, they (producers) use celery juice to sidestep consumer wariness. Unfortunately, this often means that there are more, sometimes ten times more, nitrites than conventional foods might have" (Eschliman and Ettlinger 2015, 156).

Smoke can be applied either cold, generally at 70–80°F (21–27°C), or hot, at 180°F (82°C) or higher. Smoke adds flavor, is rich in antimicrobial compounds, and has a strong antioxidative effect, which also helps deter fat from going rancid. (The "smoke ring" famously found in slowly smoked meats is not a measure of smoke penetration, but a factor of the fixative effect of smoke—nitrous oxide and carbon monoxide—on iron-containing myoglobin in the meat.)

When it comes to cured meats and charcuterie, there are some beef products included, such as the dry-cured eye of round known as bresaola, or the beef found in pepperoni and semicured sausages. There are also cured seafoods to be found, with the variety of cured salmon products leading the way. But, broadly speaking, pork is the king of cured meats. While pork's most well-known contributions include ham, bacon, most fresh sausage, and

dry-aged salami, virtually every muscle on a pig has a place in the traditional charcutier's repertoire. Michael Ruhlman and Brian Polcyn even detailed the Italian method of breaking down an entire pig in their book *Charcuterie* and dry-curing everything in *Salumi*.

When selecting pork (or any other meat) for charcuterie, buy the best and freshest meat you can find. You could certainly use a cheap, cryo-packed grocery store cut of meat with an expiration date that is somehow weeks away, and it will taste good cured or ground into sausage. But for dry-cured meats in particular, you are going to concentrate and amplify the qualities of the pork. While you might get good results from "just OK" meat, you will not make great products without great meat.

If this is your first time taking the quality of your meat seriously, the easiest thing to do may be to find a good local butcher and

Trichinosis

For generations, trichinosis was the bogeyman of pork. I was raised eating pork chops cooked to the consistency of shoe leather and moistened on the plate with apple sauce, because the USDA recommended cooking pork to a minimum of 160°F—it was commonly cooked far past that point, just to be safe.

Trichinosis, technically called trichinellosis, is a roundworm infection that occurs as a result of eating meat containing larvae of the worm trichina (*Trichinella spiralis*). It is a potential concern in flesh from animals that may be carnivorous or omnivorous, such as pigs and bears, but not herbivorous, such as deer, elk, or moose. (However, there have been stray occurrences reportedly linked to the consumption of deer.) In 2011, the USDA revised the federal guidelines for cooking pork, allowing for medium-rare pork cooked to 145°F (63°C) to be consumed. In a 2015 morbidity and mortality report surveying cases from 2008 to 2012, the CDC reported that 41 of 84 confirmed cases in that period were linked to bear meat, 10 were linked to commercial pork products, six from wild boar, and one or two each from home-raised pork, deer, and ground beef (which is sometimes mixed with pork).[*]

The rate of incidence noted in the report—a median of 15 cases a year covering the years 2008 to 2012—is an increase from the 2002 to 2007 report, but a dramatic decrease from more than 400 per year in the late 1940s. This decline dovetails with the increased widespread public concern over the safety of pork, along with legislation and widespread changes in the pork industry.

However, for meat that is not cooked at all, such as cured meat, some risk remains. Multiple strains exist, but the most commonly occurring form is *Trichinella spiralis*. *Trichinella* species that occur in pork can be eliminated with freezing; federal guidelines state that temperatures of 5°F (–15°C) or less for at least 20 days will kill any potential infection in pork that is six inches thick or less. Thinner cuts require less time on a sliding scale, as determined by the CDC.

Unfortunately, some strains that infect wild game are resistant to freeze treatment. For those interested in using wild game, especially bear meat, I would suggest using fermented sausages as an avenue. Cooking above 140°F (60°C) will eliminate the danger of consuming trichina larvae.

[*] N.O. Wilson, R.L. Hall, S.P. Montgomery, and J.L. Jones, "Trichinellosis Surveillance — United States, 2008–2012," MMWR Surveillance Summaries 64, no. SS-1 (January 16, 2015): 1–8, https://www.cdc.gov/mmwr/pdf/ss/ss6401.pdf.

just chat with them. A good butcher offering high-quality meat will not be cheap, but they can often point you in the right direction if you are looking for a less-expensive cut or are just feeling your way through new recipes and new methods. They are also more likely to offer pork from heritage breeds, which offer more flavorful meat, more and better fat, and are generally going to come from smaller operations that can afford to treat the animals much better. Aside from the ethical ramifications, you simply get better meat from animals raised in a more thoughtful, sustainable, and humane manner.

I have raised a few varieties of pigs over the years, including Berkshire, China Black, and Duroc, and have no complaints about any of them. My favorite is the Mangalitsa/ Hampshire crossbreeds I currently get from a farmer in northern Colorado. Mangalitsas are lard pigs that were originally bred in Hungary and have a thick, woolly coat. They also boast an abundance of unsaturated fat that is rich in omega-3 and omega-6 fatty acids, and a much lower melting point than animal fats higher in saturated fat. These pigs can produce great marbling and, when raised to over 300 lb. (136 kg), can have more than an inch (2.5 cm) of subcutaneous fat. During butchery we have joked about being able to cure a two-foot square piece of lardo (cured back fat).

Mangalitsa pigs, like other types of pigs that were bred for high fat content, were not just a food source; the fat was a farmhouse staple for soap, candles, machine lubricant, and home health remedies. As diets changed and populations moved from rural to urban in the first half of the twentieth century, the population of Mangalitsas dwindled until the breed was almost extinct. However, the breed has been able to rebound due to demand from small butchers and charcutiers, and they can now be sourced from farmers all over the country.

Do not get caught up on finding the "perfect" breed, though. There are many excellent types of pigs that will give you excellent results, that is, charcuterie redolent of salt, fat, spices, savoriness, and the unique flavors of the animal itself. Focus on finding quality meat. Get to know your butcher. If you can, find an outlet that offers fresh, local meat.

Prior to diving into the actual fermentation of meat, this chapter will focus on two foundational skills: dry-curing whole muscles and making fresh sausages. It is recommended that the reader be comfortable with the theory and practice of both before attempting to ferment sausages.

INTRODUCTION TO CURING

Whole-muscle curing relies on salt, as well as optional spices, sugar, and nitrate/nitrite to prevent initial surface contamination. From there, the process is a simple matter of drying the meat to a stable condition. The meat must be seasoned with at least 2.5% by weight salt and dried until it loses at least 30% of its mass. So, for every 1,000 g of meat, 25 g of salt is required, and the meat dried down to 700 g or further. Because the meat is losing moisture but not salt, the salt will concentrate to 3.5% by weight after the flesh undergoes the 30% loss. I have found that a starting level of 4% salt gives delicious results, but the reader may want to start with a lower level and work their way up to find their preferred level.

Allowing meat to lose the necessary amount of moisture is a careful balancing act. The thickness of the meat will determine how quickly it can be dried. Curing the thinner cuts of meat featured in this chapter, such as a salmon fillet or a piece of belly from a smaller pig, can be done in a regular home fridge, right next to your milk and eggs. Because the air coming in through the compressor is cold and dry, this is a low-humidity environment. Larger pieces need a dedicated chamber and careful attention to the level of humidity. This is often done with a small dorm-style fridge (i.e., a compact or mini-fridge) with a temperature regulator and a hygrometer to measure the humidity.

There are different approaches to salting meat. Brining increases the amount of water (but not necessarily the amount of flavor) in a piece of meat. Dredging or simply packing a muscle in an excess of salt for a period of time is a time-honored method, but less precise than I like. For whole muscles, my preference is to add the necessary salt based on a percentage of the meat's weight (as described above) and store the salted meat in a plastic food storage bag for a few days until the salt is fully absorbed. The salt will take additional time to transit from the exterior of the meat to the center, but this process of reaching equilibrium will continue as the meat dries, and even after that as it lies in storage prior to being eaten.

The meat might shed a little water during salting, which is not a big concern. (Or it might shed a lot if you are using mass-market grocery store meat, which is often pumped full of brine. Just another reason to steer clear of commodity meat.) After the meat takes up all of the salt, you can rub down the meat with whatever spices or herbs you choose and allow it to air dry. I recommend doing the salting and spice rub in separate stages, because I have made cured meats with both applied at the same time that have come out overly salty on the exterior. The layer of spice rub had blocked the salt from fully dissolving and being absorbed.

CURING CUTS OF MEAT AND FISH

LARDO

Lardo is possibly the simplest charcuterie to make, assuming you have access to good ingredients. It is a matter of packing a chunk of pork back fat, which is firmer than fat from other parts of the pig, in lots of salt.

Lardo is cured, but not dried. It may be difficult to find, but if you can put your hands on a piece of great back fat from an heirloom pig, this is a fantastic use for it. Because fat only contains 10%–15% water, it does not absorb salt easily and requires no drying time. However, the curing time can be months. The classic lardo is made in the Italian city of Colonnata, where it is packed in salt and stored for six months in marble containers.

I like to grab some sprigs of thyme and rosemary from the garden, making sure to distribute them on both sides of the fat. Then I simply store it away in the back of the fridge for four to six months. While I do not have marble casks at home, I have found that a zip-lock bag also works well.

Lardo is a unique addition to a charcuterie or appetizer tray. It is also remarkable when sliced thin and draped onto a slice of hot, toasted bread, possibly with a couple of basil leaves. Rich and creamy, the lardo will just melt and ooze into the bread like porcine butter.

Lardo

Ingredients
- 500 g piece of pork back fat
- 500 g (approx. 2–3 cups)* kosher salt, to cover
- 6–8 sprigs of hardy herbs, such as rosemary and thyme (optional)

*Different brands of kosher salt have differing densities, just make sure the pork is covered (see appendix A).

Directions
Put the piece of fat in a plastic food bag (black plastic, if you can find it). Distribute herbs on both sides of the fat and pour the salt over and around the fat. Put into the refrigerator for at least four months, occasionally turning over and redistributing salt.

When you are ready to consume the lardo, simply remove it from the bag and brush off any remaining salt. To store lardo, it should be wrapped in plastic and foil to minimize how much light exposure it receives. Light will cause the fat to go rancid.

CURED SALMON

Cured salmon is another very approachable entry into cured meat. Tender and dense with flavor, the salmon is not fully dried, so it is not shelf-stable, but it will last for a week to ten days, or longer if you give it some extra time to dry. Feel free to adjust the ratio of salt to sugar; many recipes call for even more sugar, but 2:1 is plenty for me. At this level it will not seem sweet, but it will take a little of the sharp edge off the saltiness.

Dry-cured salmon intensifies and enhances the flavor of the meat. It is an easy and very approachable entry into the world of curing meat.

Cured Salmon

Ingredients
- one 500 g fillet of very fresh salmon, skin-on
- 60 g salt
- 30 g sugar
- 5 g white pepper
- 15 g dill fronds
- 2 garlic cloves, smashed (optional)
- splash of gin, absinthe, or aquavit (optional)

Directions
1. Mix salt, sugar, and pepper together. Place the salmon in a plastic bag with garlic (if using) and dill laid evenly across the flesh side of the fillet. Pour half of the seasoning mixture onto each side of the salmon, and add gin, absinthe, or aquavit, if using.
2. Lay the salmon bag on a plate and put another plate on top of salmon. Using a couple of cans of food or some other weight, press the salmon between the plates and refrigerate for 2–3 days. Pull bag from between the plates once a day and redistribute seasoning as necessary.
3. After the salmon becomes firmer, remove it from the bag. Rinse and pat dry. Put salmon on a drying rack or bamboo sushi mat over a dish that will allow air to circulate above and below the salmon. Dry in the refrigerator for at least 2–3 days; the longer the salmon dries, the longer it will be shelf stable. However, the exterior of the meat will eventually dry out and form an undesirable crust on the outside of the salmon.
4. Once dried to the desired consistency, wrap the salmon in plastic. It is ready to be sliced thinly and enjoyed on a good bagel with some garlic cream cheese, or with labneh (p. 89) and spring onion kimchi (pp. 65–66).

HERB-CURED PORK BELLY

This herb-cured pork belly is a fully dry-cured variation on the Italian tradition of pancetta. Most often cooked as part of a dish, such as pasta or soup, this version is also delicious sliced thin as part of a charcuterie plate.

Herb-Cured Pork Belly

Ingredients
- one 500 g piece of pork belly, 2.5 cm (1") thick or less
- 20 g salt
- 2 g black pepper
- 2 g herbs de Provence

Directions
1. Pack the pork and salt into a plastic bag, distributing the salt over the entire surface area of the pork. Refrigerate for at least two to three days, redistributing salt once a day as necessary, until the pork has absorbed all of the salt.
2. Once all of the salt has been taken up, sprinkle half of the pepper and herbs on one side. Pat down the seasoning, flip over the pork, and add the second half of the seasoning to the other side of the belly. Press any seasoning that falls off the pork onto the sides of the belly.
3. Put the pork on a drying rack or bamboo sushi mat over a dish that will allow air to circulate above and below the pork. Allow the pork belly to air-dry in the fridge, turning over every 2–3 days, until it has dried down to 350 g or less.
4. Wrap in plastic and refrigerate once pork has reached target weight.

Cured Salmon

FRESH SAUSAGE

Sausage is a magnificent, versatile food. Sausages can be cooked, smoked, and cured; they can be grilled, sauteed, stewed, eaten on buns, and cooked into sauces, stews, and soups; they can be a main course or an ingredient that enhances a dish.

The best sausages are the ones you make, because you can use the cuts you want, the type and amount of seasoning you want, the level of heat you want. And when it comes to sausage, while other meats can and should be used in different circumstances, pork is the preeminent choice. Even if using other meats, such as chicken or venison, it is often necessary to cut the lean meat with pork fat.

Fat is elemental to the nature of sausage, and is undoubtably part of what makes sausage such an amazing food. For those who look at the recipes here and feel tempted to scale back the fat out of health concerns, I urge you not to. If you are worried about fat, eat less sausage, not sausage with less fat:

> *Too much fat tends to be the main criticism leveled at sausage, but saying you'd love sausage if only it didn't have so much fat is like saying you'd love water if only it weren't so wet. . . . If you must avoid fat for dietary reasons, avoid sausage . . . low-fat sausage is an oxymoron.* (Ruhlman and Polcyn 2005, 101)

Homemade sausage can be a canvas for your favorite herbs or spices. It offers an opportunity to create your own unique flavors, use the best ingredients, and make a product that does not include ingredients like soy protein to artificially increase the yield. Or maybe you want to dive into some cultural history by exploring traditional sausages of a given area, or pull out an old family recipe that your great-great-great grandpa used to make in the Old Country.

I rarely make a sausage that does not contain garlic, either fresh or granulated. Garlic complements almost everything. A basic sausage of garlic and pepper can be a delicious experience. Beyond that is an enormous palette of other ingredients to work with. Herbs, spices, peppers, cheese, it is all fair game. Common flavorings for sausages include black pepper, ground or chopped chile peppers, fennel seed, hardy dried herbs such as thyme, oregano, and marjoram, and sweet spices such as cloves, allspice, and cinnamon. Generally, dried spices are used at a rate of a gram to a few grams per kilogram of meat. Avoid fresh herbs when making fermented sausages, because they may carry undesirable bacteria.

In addition, large chunks of ingredients such as fruit or nuts provide a visual and textural garnish for fermented sausages that will be sliced and eaten cold. High-temperature cheeses, which are specifically labeled as such, have higher melting points (up to 400°F, or 204°C) than regular hard cheeses (~150°F, or 66°C) and make an excellent addition to smoked sausages. (High-temperature cheeses are versions of regular cheeses such as cheddar or hot pepper cheese that are specially formulated for this usage. You will not find them at your normal grocery-store cheese counter, but they can be purchased at a number of online retailers that specialize in smokehouse products.)

Small amounts of liquid can also be added to sausage to excellent effect. Rich, malty beers such as stouts, porters, brown ales, and bocks are excellent choices. Red wine is also a delicious option, or even whiskey. Liquids help by providing additional moisture to the sausage, hydrating dried spices, and helping the sausage mixture bind together. Liquid additions should be about 5%–10% volume to the weight of the sausage, or 50–100 mL per 1,000 g of sausage.

It is important to think through your flavor palette and remember that sometimes less is more. Do not try to use every spice in the cupboard; focus instead on trying to pair complementary flavors. Look at recipes for other foods and start with classic flavor combinations. Cheddar cheese might not be the ideal addition in a sausage that features Thai chiles, fish sauce, and ginger, and chipotle peppers may not pair well with herbs de Provence.

Adding dried whole milk powder to the sausage mix, at up to 32 g (¼ cup) per 1,000 g of meat, will help to retain moisture. It will also enrich and sweeten the sausage a little because of the lactose and fat in the milk, potentially tempering your spices and giving the sausage a fuller flavor. If you use dehydrated milk, just keep in mind that your sausages are not dairy free when offering them to friends (a bigger deal for commercial producers than for home sausage makers).

Each cut of meat has its own flavor nuances, but the quality of the meat is of greater importance. When formulating a pork sausage, there are plenty of recipes out there that call for different percentages of different cuts—some shoulder, some belly, some loin, some backfat—but pork shoulder is a great single piece to make sausage with. (Depending on where on the front leg it comes from and how it was cut, it may also be called pork butt, Boston butt, picnic shoulder, or picnic roast.) Shoulder has good fat content and is a flavorful cut, but you have to be careful to remove all of the sinuous connective tissue when breaking it down. For lean meats such as chicken or wild game, you will need to add back some fat to reach at least 20% fat content in your mixture. Snowy white pork fat is more aesthetically appealing than yellowish beef fat, and arguably has better flavor.

The basic stages of sausage-making include breaking down the meat, seasoning, grinding, mixing, and stuffing (also called casing). We will cover those stages here in the fresh sausage section. After that, we will add on the optional stages of fermenting, smoking, and cooking for semicured sausages.

PREPARING MEAT
FOR SAUSAGE-MAKING

To prepare meat for sausage making, it needs to be broken down into roughly 2.5 cm (1") chunks that will feed easily into your meat grinder. While breaking down the meat, be sure to remove any bloody bits for possible contamination, any soft pink or gray nodules (these are glands; they may or may not be on your cut of pork, but they can be bitter), and finally tendons and silverskin (membrane) to prevent chewy bits in your sausage.

I like to break down the meat a day in advance and refrigerate it with the salt and, if using, curing salt. This allows the salts to work into the meat and helps it to firm up prior to grinding, giving you a better, cleaner grind. I then add any other seasonings and bacterial culture just prior to the initial grind, mixing

Different types of sausage require different levels of grind. The fresh and summer sausages here are more coarsely-ground than the Lebanon bologna, which is finely ground. © Getty/golibtolibov

it evenly with the meat chunks (you can use a utensil for this or your hands, preferably with latex gloves). Seasoning the meat prior to the grind helps to distribute the seasoning and reduce how much the meat needs to be worked later on. But, in a pinch, everything can be added the day of the grind and your sausage will be fine.

The proportions of meat, fat, salt, curing salt, and bacterial culture are critical to the sausage recipe, but you have a good deal of flexibility in seasoning. A little more garlic or pepper is not going to ruin your sausage; in fact, you might prefer it. Feel free to play with different seasonings at different ratios. Just be sure to keep detailed notes in case you stumble upon a masterpiece, or if you want to get a recipe dialed in over a few iterations.

An hour or more before you plan to grind, put your seasoned meat and your grinder (or grinder parts if you have an electric model) into the freezer. It is important to have everything as cold as possible when you grind meat. You are not aiming to fully freeze the meat, but the colder and firmer it gets, the better it will grind. (This is also why salting ahead of time, essentially a quick curing, helps to improve your grind.) Aside from the risk of microbial growth, warm meat and fat will smear as it goes through the grinder, giving you a poorly textured sausage.

I began with a manual hand-cranked meat grinder that was made in Czechoslovakia. (Really. Not the Czech Republic or Slovakia. It was an old but well-crafted piece of equipment that I found online.) But a decent, brand-new electric grinder can be found these days for US$100, and a good manual grinder that was made in this century can be found for US$50 or less. You can also find grinder attachments for your stand mixer, but they can be hit-and-miss; I have heard and read too many stories about meat and fat getting mashed into a paste rather than ground. If you go that route, spend a few more bucks and look for a stainless steel one.

If you are friends with your butcher, you might also be able to get them to grind the meat for you. Buying bulk pre-ground meat is not recommended because of its unknown quality. Ground meat tends to be a catch-all for trimmings from multiple cuts of meat, resulting in a ground product of unknown constituents. It could be some shoulder, some loin, some rib meat, some sirloin, really any combination of the cuts you see available at the store.

Whatever meat grinder you buy, it should come with multiple die sizes for grinding. Grinding the meat is often done in stages, depending on the type of sausage you are making. For a standard sausage/ground meat, use the coarse (10 mm) die followed by the fine (4.5 mm) die. Some sausages call for a coarser grind, in which case you might use a medium die (6 mm). Others, especially fermented sausages that are sliced and eaten cold, benefit from having some coarse-ground fat mixed in. The large studs of fat enrich the flavor of the sausage and provide a nice visual contrast.

After grinding, the sausage blend needs to be mixed for a couple of minutes until it is sticky. Anyone who has made a lot of hamburgers has probably noticed that the more they work the meat, the stickier it becomes. Working the meat activates the protein myosin, causing it to bind to itself. Mixing the sausage blend also helps to finish distributing the salt and seasonings evenly through the meat. Prior to casing, it is common practice to cook a sample of the sausage to make sure the seasoning is right. Gently sauté a small patty (which will add Maillard and caramelization flavor) or wrap a sample in plastic and poach it for a few minutes (called the quenelle method), tasting it to make sure the seasoning is right.

CASING SAUSAGE

Whether you have an electric or hand-cranked meat grinder, it probably came with attachments to stuff sausages. If they are like the stuffer attachments I have used on grinders, they will work OK, but you will always have a bit of leftover sausage in the main chamber plus a stuffer attachment full of meat. With big enough casings you can try to cram this sausage in by hand. If you are making fermented sausage, it is helpful to keep out a little bit and age it in the same conditions as the bulk of your sausage, wrapping it in plastic or putting it in a plastic bag and using it to check the pH of your fermenting sausage. If it is fresh sausage, put it aside and use it to add punch to some pasta sauce, soup, eggs, or whatever else comes to mind.

If you find yourself regularly making sausage, eventually it becomes worthwhile to buy a separate sausage stuffer. This is generally a chamber, vertical or horizontal, that you fill with sausage and then use a follower that is fitted to the chamber to push the sausage out the other end through a stuffing tube. It is a fast and easy process. There are also attachments for stand mixers, which get mixed reviews. As is true of the grinder attachment, spend the extra money for one made of stainless steel.

You can use either natural casings or collagen casings to stuff the sausage. Natural casings need to be soaked in water to remove salt prior to use but are more pliable than collagen. They are the cleaned, scraped intestines of sheep, hogs, or cows, depending on the size you are using, which are then packed in brine to preserve them. I like to use collagen casings because they are shelf stable. I can buy a pack of a given size, usually much more than I will go through in a couple of months, and just gradually use what I need. If you have a grocery store that makes its own sausage onsite, you may be able to buy natural casings from them. Otherwise, there are a ton of options to find natural or collagen casings online. I usually use 32–38 mm casings for fresh link-type sausages such as bratwurst and 50–60 mm casings for semicured or cured sausages.

Over-stuffed sausage casings will burst when the sausage is cooked and the meat expands.

It takes some practice to learn how to stuff sausage. It often helps to have a second set of hands (and is a ripe opportunity for jokes). The casings need to be filled but not stuffed to capacity, because they will burst when the meat cooks and expands. When (not if) you have a casing rip, you can just squeeze out some sausage mix, add it back to the stuffing chamber, tie off the broken ends, and continue working. You may wind up with a stubby sausage in the batch, but it will taste just as good as the rest.

To start a new casing, tie a knot in one end of the casing and put a pinhole in the knot end of the casing. This will allow the sausage mix to fill the casing all the way to the end without creating an air bubble. Air pockets are undesirable in fresh sausage, and they can encourage microbial growth in dry-cured sausages. After you finish stuffing your sausage, be sure to go through and stick any air pockets with a pin. You can squeeze sausage down into any voids when separating the sausage into links.

Feed the open end of the casing onto the stuffer tube, planning for about 60 cm (2") of casing per 1,000 g of meat for regular link-type sausages. Fill the stuffer with sausage mix according to your equipment and operate the stuffer with one hand; when sausage mix starts coming through the stuffing tube and filling the casing, you will need to have a hand on the casing to regulate how quickly it feeds off of the stuffing tube. Too quickly and your casings will not be filled all the way, too slowly and they will get overfilled and burst immediately when linked or when cooked.

When casing sausage that will be linked, it is also important to leave a little extra capacity in the casing to allow you to separate the sausage into links. After filling a length of casing, the method I use to separate sausage links is to start at one end and measure out the length of the first link (typically 6–8" or 15–20 cm), pinch the casing between two links, and rotate the first link a couple of turns. This creates a little joint between the sausages. Then you move down to the next link and repeat the process, twisting the link in the opposite direction, creating a new joint on one side and reinforcing the previous joint on the other side. Work your way through the entire length of sausage, alternating "up" and "down" twists, and you will quickly find yourself with a pile of links where there had been a big meaty coil. I have seen a variety of "authentic" butcher's knots that can be used for tying off sausages, but I have found that a good old-fashioned square knot works just fine.

At this point, if you are making fresh sausage, you can cut the individual links apart. If you are going to hang them to smoke or otherwise cook them in a way that might allow them to untwist, then you can use cotton kitchen string to tie off the joints between links.

Remember that the sausage needs to stay cold, outside of the FDA danger zone of 40–140°F (4–60°C), as much as possible through the stuffing and linking process. Fermented sausages can start coming up to fermentation temperature after that, and fresh sausages can go into the fridge or on the grill. If you need to, take a break and cool the meat back down between grinding and stuffing. If you are making a lot of sausage you can work in batches, taking out part of it at a time to process and keeping the rest cold.

SAUSAGE PARTY: FRESH SAUSAGE RECIPES

These recipes are standardized to 1,000 g, or 1 kg (2.2 lb.). This is not an enormous batch, enough for about eight links or loose sausage for a couple of dishes. It is a good batch size to get comfortable with the process and, once you are feeling good about your methods and your recipe, it is easy to double, triple, or scale up even further.

Basic Sausage

This is the template for the remaining fresh sausages recipes in this section. When you are starting from scratch and building your own recipe, start with these ratios and extrapolate from there.

Ingredients

- 1,000 g pork shoulder (For non-pork sausages, substitute 800 g of chicken, beef, venison, or other lean meat, and 200 g pork backfat.)
- 25 g salt (2.5% of the meat weight)
- garlic, herbs, spices, peppers, cheese (these are your seasonings)
- 50–100 mL cold liquid (beer, wine, stock)

Directions

1. Cut the meat and fat into 1" (2.5 cm) cubes. Add salt to meat and let sit, refrigerated overnight, or if grinding immediately, toss with remaining seasonings and put into freezer to firm up. Freeze meat grinder.
2. Once the grinder and meat are cold, grind the sausage mixture through a coarse plate and then through a fine plate. Add liquid and mix for a couple of minutes until the seasonings are well-distributed and the mixture begins to bind.
3. Stuff sausage into 32 mm to 38 mm casings and link, or leave sausage loose.

Loose Breakfast Sausage

This is as easy as it gets and can even be made with grocery-store ground pork. It is an easy way to get a feel for how seasoning levels affect your sausage. You can cook this loose (perfect for American-style biscuits and sausage gravy), form it into patties, or stuff it into 22 mm casings.

Ingredients

- 1,000 g pork shoulder
- 25 g salt (2.5% of meat weight)
- 6.5 g black pepper
- 3 g ground ginger
- 3 g red pepper flakes
- 1 g rubbed sage
- 1 g dried thyme
- 50 g ice-cold water

Directions

1. Cut meat and fat into 1" (2.5 cm) cubes. Add salt to meat and let sit, refrigerated, overnight, or if grinding immediately, toss with remaining seasonings and put into freezer to firm up. Freeze meat grinder.
2. Once the grinder and meat are cold, grind the sausage mixture through a coarse plate and then through a fine plate. Add seasonings (if refrigerated overnight) and water; mix for a couple of minutes until seasonings are well-distributed and the mixture begins to bind.
3. Stuff sausage into 32 mm to 38 mm casings and link, or leave sausage loose.

Variation

If you substitute in 10 g fennel seed, 8 g red pepper flakes, 6 g minced garlic, 5 g dried oregano, and 3 g ground black pepper, you have got hot Italian sausage that you can use for pasta, soups, hearty stuffed eggplant, or stuff into links.

Herb and Sun-Dried Tomato Pork Sausage

Ingredients
- ❍ 1,000 g pork shoulder
- ❍ 25 g salt (2.5% of meat weight)
- ❍ 10 g garlic, minced
- ❍ 5 g black pepper
- ❍ 80 g sun-dried tomatoes, chopped finely
- ❍ 10 g blend of dried herbs, such as thyme, oregano, rosemary, and/or marjoram, chopped

Directions
1. Cut meat and fat into 1" (2.5 cm) cubes. Add salt to meat and let sit, refrigerated, overnight, or if grinding immediately, toss with remaining seasonings and put into freezer to firm up. Freeze meat grinder.
2. Once grinder and meat are cold, grind the pork through a coarse plate and then through a fine plate. Add the seasonings (if refrigerated overnight) and water; mix for a couple of minutes until seasonings are well-distributed and the mixture begins to bind.
3. Stuff sausage into 32 mm to 38 mm casings and link, or leave sausage loose.

Chicken-Bacon Sausage

The use of tequila in this sausage is a natural flavor combination with the garlic, chipotles, cumin, and some smoke from the bacon.

Ingredients
- ❍ 800 g chicken thighs
- ❍ 100 g pork backfat
- ❍ 100 g bacon, chopped finely
- ❍ 25 g salt (2.5% of meat weight)
- ❍ 20 g garlic, minced
- ❍ 100 g chipotles, chopped finely
- ❍ 10 g ground cumin
- ❍ 75 mL ice-cold tequila or chicken stock

Directions
1. Cut meat and fat into 1" (2.5 cm) cubes. Add salt to meat and let sit, refrigerated, overnight, or if grinding immediately, toss with remaining seasonings and put into freezer to firm up. Freeze meat grinder.
2. Once the grinder and meat are cold, grind the chicken and fat through a coarse plate and then through a fine plate. Add the bacon, seasonings (if refrigerated overnight), and liquid; mix for a couple of minutes until seasonings and bacon are well-distributed and the mixture begins to bind.
3. Stuff sausage into 32 mm to 38 mm casings and link, or leave sausage loose.

Fresh Sausage

© Getty/Bannibal

FERMENTED SAUSAGES

Transforming animal flesh into a shelf-stable product is a more challenging process that requires precision, but it is a tremendously rewarding experience. Whether you are camping, entertaining, or just looking for a Sunday afternoon snack, there is nothing like being able to pull out some mustard, crackers, and a hand-crafted fermented sausage. It is also a habit that can metastasize and take over parts of your life: "If you intend only to make fresh sausage for immediate consumption . . . a few tools and an afternoon are all it takes. If you decide to delve deeper, you may find your interest grow, as I have, to a consuming pastime" (Bertolli 2003, 165).

The fermentation of meat diverges from other ferments because the meat itself contains few carbohydrates for lactic-acid bacteria and yeasts to consume. As a result, the degree of fermentation and resultant level of acidity is determined by the amount of added sugar in the sausage. More sugar will result in more acidity. This factor will help define the type of sausage you are making.

Meat is a very welcoming environment to bacteria, including pathogenic bacteria, which are everywhere, waiting opportunistically for their moment to grow and multiply. Therefore, semicured sausages that are fermented, partially dried, and cooked need to reach a safe level of acidity quickly. While the interior of whole muscles from healthy animals is sterile, when you grind meat you mix any surface pathogens into the rest of the meat. Because of this, the meat you use needs to be as fresh as possible, and ground as close to when you are using it as possible. The risk is minimal for fresh sausages, which may be refrigerated for a few days and then cooked, but the risk is more significant for sausages that will spend days fermenting at room temperature or above.

Despite the measures you take to minimize bacteria, any small population of bacteria will thrive at fermentation temperature. This magnifies the importance of using the freshest, best-quality meat possible:

> When a sausage is stuffed, the only barrier that protects the meat from spoiling is salt and nitrite which were introduced during curing or mixing. The selected meat always contains some bacteria and they will grow in time. It is of the utmost importance to process meats with a bacteria count that is as low as possible. (Marianski and Marianski 2012, 37)

Along with spoilage microbes, there are microbes similar to those that are responsible for the fermentation of cheese and pickles—species of *Lactobacillus* and *Leuconostoc*—also mixed in there. This is the original basis for fermented sausage, which was originally a matter of trial and error. Whatever microbes were on the meat, casing, tools, and in the ambient environment when the sausage was made were present in the fermented sausage. From there, whatever is able to survive in a high-salt, anaerobic environment can grow and try to crowd out the competition. In some cases, beneficial bacteria achieved this by acidifying the sausage environment, creating relatively stable, slightly tart sausages whose descendants include summer sausage and other regional variations. Sandor Katz describes this in *The Art of Fermentation*, "As in most fermentations, the environment selects the bacteria. The hard part is creating the appropriate environment, not getting the bacteria there" (Katz 2012, 350).

Prior to an understanding of microbiology and the availability of pure bacterial cultures, *backslopping* was widely used to maintain quality and consistency in a variety of fermented products. Backslopping is a method that simply involves adding back part of a previous successful fermentation—brine, whey, meat from a batch of sausage—to the new batch. Though the microbial context was not understood at the time, this allowed low-tech fermented food producers to keep a successful microbial culture or set of cultures active, rather than rolling the dice and starting over with every new batch. It also helped to isolate specific "house" characters; over many generations of bacteria, the culture in a certain producer's meat or cheese would evolve and adapt to the producer's unique environment, much as a brewer's yeast will continue to evolve over many years in isolation at a given brewery.

However, because backslopping is ultimately less reliable and less accurate than modern pure cultures, and carries forward any undesirable microbial populations from a previous batch, it is not generally used for fermenting food today. Nowadays, bacterial cultures are isolated, grown up in quantity, then dried to preserve them.

Fermented sausage bacteria are lactic acid producers, closely related to the bacteria we rely on for cheese and vegetable acidification. (They can also create trace amounts of alcohol, acetic acid, and flavor-active compounds.) However, some species, including *Lactobacillus brevis* and *Leuconostoc mesenteroides*, which are used in other types of fermentation, are undesirable in sausage because they can produce overly sour sausages and create carbon dioxide (Marianski and Marianski 2012, 32). Because of this, it is not recommended to try to cross-ferment meat with cheese or pickle cultures. It is worth the expense to get the right culture for your application and not cut open your sausage to find a Swiss-cheese mosaic of CO_2 holes.

There are a few different options for fermenting sausages, depending on your conditions. Bactoferm F-RM-52 from Chr. Hansen, containing *Lactobacillus sakei* and *Staphylococcus carnosus*, is a standard choice for sausages fermented above 70°F (21°C). Bactoferm F1, containing *Pediococcus pentosaceus* and *Staphylococcus xylosus*, is a fast-fermenting culture that can also be used, and Bactoferm LHP is an extra-fast option for temperatures above 80°F (27°C). Bactoferm F-LC can be used for fast fermentation above 100°F (38°C) and also produces bacteriocins, proteins that inhibit the growth of *Listeria monocytogenes*.

Try to find a warm, moist location to ferment your sausages. That may be in a cooler with jars of warm water, or in your stove with the light left on and a bowl of warm water for humidity. If you want to step up the level of technical precision, an aquarium heating pad can be used in a cooler and powered through a temperature controller. You may need to keep the cooler cracked or periodically open it to vent moisture to keep the ambient humidity below 90%.

Before you first put away your sausages to ferment, you may also need to let them sit out and come to room temperature, called tempering. If you have done a good job keeping your meat cold and have cold sausages ready to ferment, they may become coated with condensation if they go straight into the warm chamber. This moisture will encourage the development of surface mold. If your sausages do start to collect some condensate, leave them in a warm, low-humidity space with minimal airflow until they come up to room temperature.

Fermentation should start at around 90% or greater humidity to prevent moisture loss, however, humidity that is too high—often the result of a closed chamber without enough airflow—can lead to undesirable mold forming on the surface of the sausage. Humidity in the fermentation chamber can slowly drop as fermentation finishes and the sausage begins to dry.

Too much drying at this stage can impair fermentation, which will slow or stall below water activity (a_w) of 0.95. Fermentation will continue until the sugar is fully consumed, the a_w drops too far, or the temperature below 50°F (10°C). If you find that the sausage has reached the target pH, it can be refrigerated to stop fermentation. For your first batches, start at the lower end of acidity (i.e., a slightly higher pH), while still calculating to finish around pH 5.0, and keeping an eye on the acidity level in your plastic-wrapped sample. If you find that more acidity is desirable or if your sausage is not reaching the desired level of fermentation, then you can increase the amount of sugar used to feed your culture.

Keep in mind that, depending on other conditions, fermentation can continue until all of the available sugar is consumed. Some sausage cultures can tolerate a pH as low as 3.0, and some may continue fermenting slowly with temperatures in the low 50s Fahrenheit (10–13°C), so the best way to control your pH is by calibrating the amount of sugar you add to the sausage mix.

Fermento can also be used as a substitute for fermentation. A dairy-based product offered by The Sausage Maker, Fermento will acidify your sausage immediately. It is not a bacterial culture itself, but a product of bacterial fermentation that eliminates the need for a longer fermentation time. Sausages made with Fermento can be smoked, cooked, or dried immediately after stuffing.

Calculating Sugar or Fermento Addition

The amount of sugar, if fermenting your sausage, or Fermento you add will determine the level of acidity in your finished sausage. Because you can see different pH values even from the same cut from different animals, and liquid additions such as beer or wine will affect the starting pH of your sausage, you should measure the pH after it has been ground and loosely mixed and calculate your dextrose addition.

For fermentation using bacteria and dextrose, the Marianskis recommend as a general rule that 0.1% dextrose (i.e., 1 g per 1 kg of meat) will lower the pH of meat by about 0.1 pH; 1% will drop the meat a full pH unit, for example from 6.0 to 5.0 or 5.5 to 4.5 (Marianski and Marianski 2012, 128). A common level to add is 0.5–0.7%, which will ferment the meat to just below pH 5.0.

For bacterial cultures, usage rates will vary slightly between different cultures, but in general a 25–50 g package of dried culture will ferment hundreds of pounds or kilograms of meat. For practical purposes, a ¼ teaspoon of culture in a batch is more than strictly necessary but is enough to handle easily and will ensure that the bacteria is distributed throughout the batch.

If using Fermento, start with an addition of 3%, which should lower your sausage pH to about 5.0. For a tangier sausage, Fermento can be used at up to 6%, but beyond that level it will start to degrade the meat.

While the content of lactic acid in fully dry-cured sausages such as salami is a small factor in its preservation and safety, semicured sausages rely heavily on fermentation for preservation and so need to reach a safe pH of 5.3 in a matter of days. While fermented sausages will often drop farther than this, pH 5.3 is considered a relatively stable product. How long a sausage takes to reach pH 5.3 is one benchmark the USDA uses to determine its level of safety.

Fermentation proceeds faster at higher temperatures, but so does the growth of other bacteria. As a result, the USDA Food Safety and Inspection Service uses a measure called "degree-hours" to calculate if a semidry or semicured sausage was produced safely. This serves as a proxy measure to limit the potential for pathogenic bacteria to reproduce. One degree-hour is equal to one hour at one degree above 60°F. So, one hour at 65°F or five hours at 61°F both equal 5 degree-hours. Federal guidelines limit the number of degree-hours that a sausage can take to reach a safe pH of 5.3 and a loss of 15% moisture to a maximum of 1,200 degree-hours. I like to start with my fermentation temperature, then back-calculate the allowable time at that temperature:

$$\text{time limit (hours)} = \frac{1,200 \text{ °F-hours}}{T_{\text{ferm.}} \text{ (in °F)} - 60\text{°F}}$$

For example, if I am fermenting at the low end, 75°F, I calculate

$$\text{time limit} = \frac{1,200 \text{ °F-hours}}{75\text{°F} - 60\text{°F}}$$

$$= \frac{1,200 \text{ °F-hours}}{15\text{°F}}$$

$$= 80 \text{ hours}$$

This means that my sausage can take up to 80 hours to drop to a pH of 5.3 and be considered safe.

Similarly, if I am fermenting at 90°F, my calculations look like:

$$\text{time limit} = \frac{1,200 \text{ °F-hours}}{90\text{°F} - 60\text{°F}}$$

$$= \frac{1,200 \text{ °F-hours}}{=30\text{°F}}$$

$$= 40 \text{ hours}$$

So, at 90°F, knowing that my fermentation culture and the pathogenic bacteria will both be reproducing at an accelerated rate, I have half as much time as I would at 75°F to reach a safe pH and moisture loss. If your sausages take longer than 1,200 degree-hours to ferment and dry to a safe point (they may continue to ferment as long as necessary after hitting 5.3 pH), then you risk having elevated populations of *E. coli*, listeria, salmonella, or other dangerous bacteria, and should dispose of the batch rather than rolling the dice with your health.

When calculating your sugar addition for meat fermentations, be sure to use dextrose rather than other types of sugar. A form of glucose, dextrose

Measuring pH

Hang on to the scraps from your sausage stuffer, they can be used to monitor the fermentation in your sausages.

The advanced homebrewer may already have a pH meter in their arsenal already. If not, a decent one can be purchased for about US$50; make sure it comes with calibration solutions, or purchase them along with your meter, and follow the calibration instructions that come with your pH meter. A good pH meter that is not calibrated is not really giving you useful or accurate information. pH strips are also available, but be sure to get strips with a narrow range to get the most accurate reading. Strips that cover most of the range for beer—4.6 to 6.2 pH—are readily available.

When you finish casing a batch, wrap the leftover sausage in plastic and ferment it with the rest of your batch. To monitor the progress of your fermentation, simply pull a small sample of your plastic-wrapped scraps and mix two parts distilled water to one part sausage. Test it with your meter or a pH strip, being careful not to contact the strip with sausage solids that may discolor the strip.

Testing the pH of your fermented sausage is crucial to ensuring the safety of the sausage.

can be metabolized by all types of bacteria you will come across for fermenting sausages. Table sugar, on the other hand, can be troublesome for certain strains of bacteria. A mix of fructose and glucose, table sugar may ferment more slowly because the bacteria have to cleave the sucrose molecules into their constituent sugars before metabolizing them into lactic acid.

To ensure proper distribution in the meat, combine the starter culture with a small amount (¼–½ cup, 60–120 mL) of chlorine-free water. Otherwise, the addition is so small that it may not be adequately mixed through the entire batch.

A safe pH is a crucial target to hit, but it is not the only factor that ensures the safety of your fermented sausage. In general, fermented foods do not usually reach an optimal point of safety based on a single factor (i.e., salinity, pH, a_w or moisture loss), but often operate on the idea that each factor is detrimental to the bacterial population, and multiple hurdles can tag-team pathogenic bacteria to keep food safe.

Another variable that is used to control bacterial growth, as mentioned in the USDA guidelines, is the level of moisture available (i.e.,

water activity, or a_w, which I will discuss shortly). While the USDA allows for sausages to be considered shelf stable when they reach either 0.85 a_w or pH 4.6, most fermented sausages rely on a combination of factors that also include salt, nitrates, smoking, and cooking. The Marianskis comment that most American semidry sausages reach pH 4.8 or lower (Marianski and Marianski 2012, 128). Depending on your ending pH, your sausage may have a noticeable tang. This can be softened by the addition of unfermentable sugars such as dry milk (lactose) as described in the fresh sausage section (p. 126).

Meat is such a receptive environment for bacteria because it is 75% water, and the vast majority of that water is not bound up chemically. The degree to which water is available is referred to as water activity (a_w), which is a measure between 1.0 (100% of moisture is available) and 0 (absolute bone dry, or all moisture is chemically bound). It is a measure of the water that is available to react with. Salt and sugar, for example, bond with water and make it unavailable without removing it from the meat. (For more on a_w and the susceptibility of pathogenic bacteria to a_w levels, see p. 9.)

An initial salting drops the a_w of ground meat from 0.99 (it is not 1.0 because a small amount of the water present in the meat is bound up in protein and other constituents) to between 0.96 and 0.98, according to Marianski and Marianski (2012, 16). It may seem like a small difference, but a change in a_w of a couple hundredths immediately creates a less hospitable environment for bacteria. Spoilage bacteria, which break down meat into slimy, mushy, foul-smelling rot, are generally inactive below 0.97 a_w. However, sausage cultures slow down when a_w drops to 0.95 (Marianski and Marianski 2012, 32). As a result, it is important to keep the fermenting sausage from drying too quickly.

Commercial producers will often use an a_w meter, which can cost hundreds of dollars. For home production, the percentage of weight loss is a reasonable substitute. As noted before, 15% loss is a lower limit for fermented sausages, while fully dry-cured sausages can lose 30% or more. This means that for every 1,000 g (i.e., one kilogram) of sausage you start with, you finish with 850 g or less of fermented sausage. The water content of the meat drops from 75% to around 40%–50%, while the salt concentration rises from 2.5% to about 3.5%.

Remember that these targets, pH 5.3 and 15% moisture loss, are minimums. Some experimentation may lead you to decide that you prefer increased moisture loss and a lower pH. Do not be afraid to go to 20% moisture loss or more, which will concentrate the flavors further and give you a denser product. And keep in mind that if you smoke the sausages, hot or cold, that will strip away some additional moisture, which may take you from 15% loss to more than 20%.

While drying should take place near the end of or after fermentation to prevent the bacteria from going inactive, the Marianskis point out that it is easier to dry sausages after fermentation (Marianski and Marianski 2012, 43). As the level of acidity rises and pH falls, it pushes the meat to the isoelectric point of its constituent proteins, generally between pH 4.8 and 5.3, where the water in the sausage is more weakly bonded and able to evaporate more easily. If your sausage has not lost the desired amount of moisture by the end of fermentation (as long as the loss has been at least 15%), you can hang it in a cool basement, garage, or leave it on a rack in the refrigerator for a few days prior to smoking and/or cooking.

Another factor to consider in the safe preservation of your sausages is the inclusion of curing salt. Known variously as Prague Powder, Insta Cure #1, TCM (Tinted Cure Mix), or pink salt, curing salt is a pink-tinted mixture that consists of 6.25% sodium nitrite and sodium chloride. Curing salt is necessary to restrain the growth of *Clostridium botulinum* in preserved sausages. It is important to only use Cure #1 for faster fermented sausages; Cure #2 contains a blend of sodium nitrite and sodium nitrate, which requires time and slow bacterial activity to convert to nitrite. This conversion will not occur in the time available for fermentations that are supposed finish in less than a week.

While nitrite in fermented meat dissipates over time, its presence is essential to create safe initial conditions in preserved ground-meat products. Early on in my curing days, I had a batch of sausage, possibly made with meat purchased from a major national grocer and "enhanced" with a certain percentage of injected brine solution, that had a ton of moisture separate out while the ground meat was sitting with salt. I poured off the moisture, cased the sausage, and cured it. When I finally went to taste it after dry-curing, I realized that the excess moisture had carried away a large portion of the salt, and probably a lot of the nitrates as well. It went straight into the trash. Better safe than sorry; no need to roll the dice on botulism.

SMOKING AND COOKING

Once your sausage has finished fermenting, it is ready for some smoke or it can be finished by roasting or poaching gently. (If you are going straight to cooking, skip down a few paragraphs.) Semidry sausages from central and southern Europe, countries such as Spain, France, Italy, and Hungary, generally have mold on the exterior, while northern and eastern European countries such as Germany, Poland, Russia, UK, and the Scandinavian bloc tend toward smoked sausages (Marianski and Marianski 2012, 36).

Cold smoking is done at a temperature that will not melt fat or cook the sausage but imparts the flavor and other benefits of smoke; this is generally around 70°F (21°C). In addition to flavor enhancement, cold smoking also facilitates drying, allows fermentation to continue, and adds a layer of antimicrobial action to the sausage, helping to prevent mold formation. Cold smoking is not just for meat; it is also an excellent method to impart smoke flavor to cheeses, nuts, or a variety of other foods that may not benefit from cooking. Cold smoking can be difficult, because it requires a way to cool the smoke as it travels from the fire to the food. This is often done on a professional scale by having a separate fire pit that is ducted into a smoking chamber some distance away, allowing the smoke to cool to ambient temperature along the way. On a small scale, you could run a pipe or tube from the chimney of your smoker to a separate chamber, or place a tray of ice between the fire box and the food. One of my smokers consists of two steel drums stacked and welded together, with a door on the bottom to build a fire and a door on the top to hang sausages. I like to build a small fire in the smoker in the evening—especially in the fall and winter when the weather will keep the temperature in check—hang the sausages, and close up the smoker overnight, giving them a cool all-night smoke. Then the fire can be stoked in the morning to finish cooking them through.

Hot smoking at 180–250°F (93–121°C) infuses the food with smoke while also slowly heating it to cooking temperature. If you find the fat in your sausage is rendering or squirting out, your smoker is running too hot. Cold smoking followed by a gradual temperature increase is an excellent way to get plenty of smoke flavor and cook the meat. Whatever method you use, it is important that the food is fairly dry to the touch but still slightly tacky when it goes into the smoker. This surface condition, called a pellicle, allows the smoke to bond better with the food. Food with excess moisture on the surface does not pick up as much smoke flavor. When hanging sausages to smoke, any surface that makes contact with another sausage, the smoker, or the hanging device will not get smoked. It will get cooked, if that is part of your aim, but it will not pick up any coloration from the smoking process.

Gentle smoking is important to prevent the sausages taking on an acrid flavor, but 8–12 hours of cold smoking (or less, depending on your preference and the intensity of your smoke) can impart excellent character. The type of wood you use for smoking will have a profound effect on the sausage. Lump oak charcoal is my go-to, often with some fruit wood, which is sweeter and more delicate. Hickory and mesquite also produce delicious and strongly flavored smoke. Hickory is widely used for smoking, while mesquite is generally associated with Texas-style barbecue.

A variety of other woods are used for smoking in the United States and around the world, including pecan, maple, alder, beech, and juniper. You can explore other woods that may be available to you, but avoid soft woods such as pine, spruce, or cedar. Because they contain a higher proportion of terpenes and sap, smoking with soft woods can lead to an unpleasant, resinous smoke and can potentially sicken people who eat the meat. Be sure to do your research when considering a new smoke source; there are even some hardwoods that should be avoided. It goes without saying that **treated lumber cannot be used for smoking.**

If you are skipping the smoking stage or only using cold smoke, your sausages can be finished in the oven or on the stovetop. Bake at 200°F (93°C), or poach the sausages gently in barely-simmering water. Pork and beef should be cooked to an internal temperature of at least 150°F (66°C) and poultry to 165°F (74°C). Dropping the sausages into an ice bath or rinsing them with cold water after cooking, contrary to what you might think, does not remove flavor, aside from some trace smoke on the casing. Rather, it will prevent the sausage from cooling slowly and shriveling up. You have undoubtably seen hot dogs or sausages that came off of a grill a couple of hours earlier and, as they gradually drop to room temperature, become shrunken, wrinkly, sad-looking vestiges of what they were.

SAUSAGE PARTY REDUX: FERMENTED SAUSAGE RECIPES

Smoked Kielbasa

Ingredients

- 1,000 g pork shoulder
- 25 g salt (2.5% of meat weight)
- 2.5 g Cure #1 (0.25%)
- 2 g black pepper
- 1 large garlic clove, minced (about 4 g)
- 0.5 g dried marjoram
- 125 mL ice-cold water or stock

Directions

1. Cut meat and fat into 2.5 cm (1") cubes. Add salt and Cure #1 to the meat and let sit, refrigerated overnight, or if grinding immediately, toss with remaining seasonings and put into freezer to firm up. Freeze meat grinder.

2. Once grinder and meat are cold, grind the sausage mixture through a coarse plate and then through a medium plate. Add remaining seasonings (if refrigerated overnight) and water; mix for a couple of minutes until seasonings are well-distributed and the mixture begins to bind.

3. Stuff sausage into 32 mm casings. Smoke gently until the internal temperature reaches at least 150°F (71°C). Cool in an ice bath and refrigerate.

Kielbasa

© Getty/rudisill

Dunkelwurst

Finally, this is our first real fermented sausage recipe. The addition of a high proportion of nice malty lager, like a good German-style dunkel, rounds out the flavor profile of the sausage, and is especially good smoked. This recipe makes three sausage loops of 12–15" (30–38 cm).

A rich, malty beer in this sausage helps to offset a hearty dose of spice from the black pepper, red pepper, mustard, onion, and garlic.

Ingredients

- 565 g beef
- 310 g pork
- 125 g pork fat
- 25 g salt (2.5% of meat weight)
- 2.5 g Cure #1 (0.25%)
- 6 g black pepper
- 3.5 g granulated garlic
- 2.8 g dried onion
- 5 g red pepper flakes
- 1.5 g ground mustard
- 1.9 g ground thyme
- 125 mL ice-cold dunkel or other malty beer
- ¼ tsp sausage culture plus sugar, or Fermento

Directions

1. Cut meat and fat into 2.5 cm (1") cubes. Add salt and nitrate to meat and let sit, refrigerated, overnight, or if grinding immediately, toss with remaining seasonings and put into freezer to firm up. Freeze meat grinder.

2. Once the grinder and meat are cold, grind the sausage mixture through a coarse plate and then through a medium plate. Add remaining seasonings (if refrigerated overnight) and beer and give an initial mix. Test the pH of your sausage mix and calculate your sugar addition for fermentation or your Fermento addition (see p. 134).

3. Stuff sausage into 32mm casings. Ferment to below 5.3 pH in 1,200 degree-hours or fewer, as described above, or if using Fermento, sausage can be hung to dry and then cooked, or cooked immediately.

4. Depending on how much it is dried, sausage can stay good for weeks to months in the refrigerator.

Elk summer sausage

Summer sausage is a great way to use some of the lean game meat that comes from being a hunter. The elk in this recipe can be swapped out for venison or lean beef. To make it with chicken, use chicken thighs, which are fattier and juicier. However, chicken has a higher pH, usually 6.0 or above. Because of this, you will need additional sugar to ferment to a safe pH, and it is recommended that the amount of culture be doubled to help reduce the initial lag time and kick-start fermentation.

These summer sausage recipes are scaled to fit the 2 ft. (60 cm) long, 60 mm collagen casings commonly available. One recipe of about 1,250 to 1,300 grams of meat and fat will fill a single 2 ft. casing.

© Getty/Nancybelle Gonzaga Villarroya

Ingredients
- 1,000 g elk, venison, or other lean meat
- 250 g pork backfat
- 31.25 g salt (2.5% of meat weight)
- 3.125 g Cure #1 (0.25%)
- 8.6 g black pepper
- 6.5 g whole mustard seeds
- 6.5 g granulated garlic
- 6.5 g ground ginger
- 1.5 g dried marjoram
- 1.5 g dried thyme
- 2 g ground allspice
- 75 mL ice-cold liquid
- ¼ tsp sausage culture plus sugar, or Fermento

Directions
1. Cut the meat and fat into 2.5 cm (1") cubes. Add salt and nitrate to the meat and let sit, refrigerated, overnight, or if grinding immediately, toss with remaining seasonings and put into freezer to firm up. Freeze meat grinder.

2. Once grinder and meat are cold, grind the sausage mixture through a coarse plate and then through a medium plate. Add remaining seasonings (if refrigerated overnight) and water and give an initial mix. Test the pH of your sausage mix and calculate your sugar addition for fermentation or your Fermento addition (see p. 134).

3. Optional: Half of the fat can be put aside after being ground through the coarse plate and mixed back into the ground sausage mix. This fat will lend a nice visual contrast to the finished sausage.

4. Stuff sausage into 60 mm casings. Ferment to below pH 5.3 in 1,200 degree-hours or fewer (p. 134); or if using Fermento, the sausage can be hung to dry and then cooked, or cooked immediately.

5. Depending on how much it is dried, the sausage can stay good in the fridge for weeks to months.

Cheddar-Jalapeño Summer Sausage

When you are mixing in the cheese and jalapeños here it will seem like an excessive amount, but you are looking for both flavor and the visual contrast the green peppers provide when studded through the meat in every slice. If you can find high-temperature cheese, it will also add a nice visual element to the sausage; but, if not, regular cheddar will still add good flavor to the sausage.

Walnuts, cranberries, jalapeños, and high-temperature cheese add a visual contrast to fermented sausages.

Ingredients

- ○ 1,000 g beef top round
- ○ 250 g pork backfat
- ○ 31.25 g salt (2.5% of meat weight)
- ○ 3.125 g Cure #1 (0.25%)
- ○ 7.5 g black pepper
- ○ 0.55 tbsp garlic powder
- ○ 250 g sharp cheddar cheese, shredded or cut into small cubes
- ○ four to six fresh jalapeños, chopped
- ○ 0.5 tsp dried marjoram
- ○ ¼ tsp sausage culture plus sugar, or Fermento

Directions

1. Cut meat and fat into 2.5 cm (1") cubes. Add salt and nitrate to meat and let sit, refrigerated, overnight, or if grinding immediately, toss with remaining seasonings and put into freezer to firm up. Freeze meat grinder.
2. Once grinder and meat are cold, grind the sausage mixture through a coarse plate and then through a fine plate. Add remaining seasonings (if refrigerated overnight) and water and give an initial mix. Test the pH of your sausage mix and calculate your sugar addition for fermentation or your Fermento addition (see p. 134).
3. Stuff sausage into 60 mm casings. Ferment to below pH 5.3 in 1,200 degree-hours or fewer (p. 134); or if using Fermento, the sausage can be hung to dry and then cooked, or cooked immediately.
4. Depending on how much it is dried, the sausage can stay good in the fridge for weeks to months.

Fall Sausage

This fall sausage recipe is a version of a smoked sausage I first made years ago for Thanksgiving. Featuring sage, walnuts, and dried cranberries, it was the perfect midday bite to hold us over until the turkey came off the smoker.

Ingredients
- 1,800 g beef top round
- 450 g pork backfat
- 56 g salt (2.5% of meat weight)
- 5.6 g Cure #1 (0.25%)
- 8 g black pepper
- 0.75 g dried marjoram
- 0.75 g dried thyme
- 2 g ground nutmeg
- 50 g (1½ cups) dried cranberries
- 90 g (¾ cup) chopped walnuts
- ¼ tsp sausage culture, plus sugar or Fermento

Directions
1. Cut meat and fat into 2.5 cm (1") cubes. Add salt and nitrate to meat and let sit, refrigerated, overnight, or if grinding immediately, toss with remaining seasonings and put into freezer to firm up. Freeze meat grinder.
2. Once grinder and meat are cold, grind the sausage mixture through a coarse plate and then through a medium plate. Add remaining seasonings (if refrigerated overnight) and water and give an initial mix. Test the pH of your sausage mix and calculate your sugar addition for fermentation or your Fermento addition (see p. 134).
3. Stuff sausage into 60 mm casings. Ferment to below pH 5.3 in 1,200 degree-hours or fewer (p. 134); or if using Fermento, the sausage can be hung to dry and then cooked, or cooked immediately.
4. Depending on how much it is dried, the sausage can stay good in the fridge for weeks to months.

Lebanon Bologna

Lebanon bologna is a spectacular product from Lebanon, Penn., not at all like the bologna you probably grew up with. Smoked (there is even a double-smoked variety) beef sausage, finely ground and speckled with fat, seasoned with sweet spices, and not emulsified like that other "baloney."

This recipe is scaled for one 2 ft. (60 cm) 120 mm casing, generally used for large-diameter deli meats, but it can be scaled down for smaller casings.

Ingredients
- 3.5 kg beef chuck
- 88 g salt (2.5% of meat weight)
- 8.75 g Cure #1 (0.25%)
- 10 g ground black pepper
- 7 g ground allspice
- 3.5 g ground cinnamon
- 3.5 g ground cloves
- 2 g ground ginger
- ¼ tsp sausage culture, plus sugar or Fermento

Directions
1. Cut meat and fat into 2.5 cm (1") cubes. Add salt and nitrate to meat and let sit, refrigerated, overnight, or if grinding immediately, toss with remaining seasonings and put into freezer to firm up. Freeze meat grinder.
2. Once grinder and meat are cold, grind the sausage mixture through a coarse plate and then through a fine plate. Add remaining seasonings (if refrigerated overnight) and water and give an initial mix. Test the pH of your sausage mix and calculate your sugar addition for fermentation or your Fermento addition (see p. 134).
3. Stuff sausage into 120 mm casings. Ferment to below pH 5.3 in 1,200 degree-hours or fewer (p. 134); or if using Fermento, the sausage can be hung to dry or smoked immediately.
4. Once fermented and ready to cook, hang the sausage in a cold smoker overnight. The next morning, feed the fire and slowly smoke until internal temperature reaches 150°F (66°C). Cool in ice bath and refrigerate.

APPENDIX A

SALT

Salt is a cornerstone of food preservation, including many preservation methods that involve fermentation. Pickled vegetables, cheese, and cured meats all rely on salt. It draws out moisture and holds undesirable microbial growth at bay, clearing the way for beneficial bacteria to take over and thrive. Many of the foods in this book could not exist without salt. Nor could human life.

As Ruhlman and Polcyn put it, "Without the mineral sodium chloride, our muscles would cease to function, our organs would starve. Because our body doesn't produce it and because we need it to survive, humans developed a distinct sense for salt, and our bodies are highly attuned to the need for salt" (2005, 30). Salt regulates fluid exchange in our cells, which results in nutrients being able to enter them. It is the rock that we need to survive.

For thousands of years, humanity has recognized the value of salt. Salt, saltworks, and the salt economy have helped define human history and culture, ranging from the ancient Chinese, Egyptian, and Roman civilizations up through the American Revolutionary War and the American Civil War. The Chinese had discovered salting meat as a way to preserve it before 2,200 BC, while Egyptians had learned the method by 1,500 BC (Marianski and Marianski 2008, 11). The Chinese and Roman empires manipulated salt prices and controlled production as a revenue source.

The word *soldier* is descended from the Latin *sal* ("salt"), via the French *solde* (meaning "pay"), according to Mark Kurlansky: "At times, [Roman] soldiers were even paid in salt, which was the origin of the word salary and the expression 'worth his salt' or 'earning his salt'" (2002, 63). The salting of cod and other fish fueled Viking and European explorers; Germanic tribes 2,000 years ago thought that the gods would listen more closely to their prayers if they were made in a salt mine. Without knowing why, people eventually realized that salt from different mines would cure meat differently, in some cases imparting a unique flavor and preserving the meat for longer, eventually leading to the use of saltpeter (potassium nitrate), the original nitrate used for curing.

Over the last 100 to 150 years (fairly recent in the grand scheme of humanity), the practice of salt-preserving foods out of necessity gave way to freezing and canning technology. But many of these foods have survived modernization, not because the average American still needs to pack away meat and vegetables in salt to ride out a hard winter, but because of the flavor. A taste for salt and the amplified flavors that often go with it—acidity in pickles, savory meatiness in charcuterie, creamy fattiness in cheese—are hardwired into our brains. Even those food types that do not require salt, such as bread, would simply be less delicious without it.

Technically, a salt is any substance that is the result of an acid–base reaction, and examples of salts include sodium chloride, sodium carbonate, calcium chloride, and magnesium chloride, among thousands of others. Salts form when a positive ion (cation), which needs an electron, combines with an anion (negative ion), which has an excess of electrons. In sodium chloride (what we commonly refer to as "salt"), the sodium ion is the cation and chloride is the anion. Kurlansky notes:

> It turns out that salt was a microcosm for one of the oldest concepts of nature and the order of the universe. From the fourth century BC Chinese belief in the forces of yin and yang, to most of the world's religions, to modern science, to the basic principles of cooking, there has always been a belief that two opposing forces find completion—one receiving a missing part and the other shedding an extra one. A salt is a small but perfect thing. (2002, 300).

For our purposes, salt refers to table salt, kosher salt, sea salt, any variety of food-grade sodium chloride. Although I touch on the use of nitrates (curing salts) and calcium chloride in various places in the book, I do not refer to them as "salt."

One of the most unique aspects of salt is its ability to penetrate into food, as compared to other spices and seasonings that sit on the surface of the food. Sodium chloride dissolves in water into separate, single ions of sodium (Na^+) and chloride (Cl^-), which are smaller than food molecules and can pass through cell walls, reacting with proteins and pulling moisture out via osmosis. Additional trace minerals or additives in the salt can also affect the fermented food.

Strictly speaking, all salt comes from the sea, whether modern seas that give us "sea salt," or ancient seas that left behind salt deposits that are now mined and processed to give us other types of salt (e.g., kosher, pickling, and iodized salt). Unrefined or minimally refined salt is generally recommended for all of the methods and food types in this book. This includes sea salt, kosher salt, or pickling salt. However, no two sources of unrefined salt are the same, and many will not naturally contain enough calcium in their trace minerals to produce crisper pickles. This is why I recommend in the pickling chapter of the book adding a healthy pinch of calcium chloride. Sea salt is made from evaporated sea water, and different grades will have different properties. *Sel gris*, or gray salt, contains trace minerals, clay, and other sediments. *Fleur de sel* is a finer grade of sea salt that consists of delicate crystals.

Pickling salt or canning salt—and cheese salt, which is very similar—is very fine-grained so that it will dissolve quickly, but is also refined to remove trace minerals. Kosher salt is named for its original use, to purify meat by drawing out the blood, rather than some unique composition or manufacturing. Kosher salt is made of coarser grains and, unlike most table salt, is not iodized. Kosher salt is usually my go-to salt for cooking, because the larger grains allow for me to easily grab the oft-needed "pinch" of salt.

However, it is refined to remove other minerals, and some brands of kosher salt contain anticaking agents, which can lead to a cloudy pickle brine. Table salt—which is frequently iodized—is highly refined salt, whereby the trace minerals are stripped out and potassium iodide, stabilizers, and anticaking agents are added back in. Iodized salt is not recommended for fermentation because the iodine can inhibit microbial activity and can lend a metallic taste. The stabilizers and anticaking agents can leave you with a cloudy brine.

There are also boutique unrefined salts on the market that are more expensive but may not offer much more in terms of flavor or performance as a preservative. Himalayan pink salt contains trace minerals that color it, while Hawaiian black salt is a mix of sea salt and volcanic charcoal. When considering a top-shelf salt for pickling or curing, keep in mind that the salt is almost entirely sodium chloride. The other trace components may have a very minor impact on the final product when you consider the price of the salt.

Anyone who has access to different types of salt will notice quickly that they vary in physical form, from large flakes to fine crystals to coarse grains. As a result, the same volume of different salts will give you different weights of salt. A teaspoon of coarse sea salt does not equal a teaspoon of pickling salt. Because of this, recipes in this book are based on weight. Having the right balance of salt is crucial to the quality of your fermented foods. An inadequate balance will lead to the growth of undesirable microbes and, eventually, to rot. A high level of salt will dehydrate cells through osmosis, removing moisture from the meat or vegetable, dehydrating spoilage and pathogenic bacteria in the process. Too much salt will make the food unpalatable and, at a certain point, impede the growth of your desired microbes.

So, if too much salt is bad for the microbes, how bad is it for humans? As with most medical questions, the answer is complicated and continues to evolve. Kurlansky notes that scientists are still debating how much salt an adult needs to be healthy, with estimates ranging from about 300 g (⅔ lb.) to more than 7.25 kg (over 16 lb.) *per year* (Kurlansky 2002, 9). Some of this variability is the result of different geographic needs. People who live in hotter regions sweat more, losing salt in the process, and simply need to consume more salt to replace it. However, most of the difference lies in the vagaries of research on human biology.

The *daily* sodium intake recommended by the CDC is less than 2,300 mg, or 2.3 g.[1] Most Americans regularly exceed that, at an average of 3,400 mg per day. (Since sodium chloride consists of 40% sodium by weight, sodium content can be converted to salt by multiplying by 2.5, and salt can be converted to sodium by multiplying by 0.4.)

While few, if any, researchers oppose the idea that lowering salt levels can improve blood pressure for hypertensive individuals, the benefit for healthy adults is much less pronounced. A meta-analysis of studies involving reduced-sodium diets that lasted at least six months showed a reduction of 1 mmHg for systolic blood pressure and less than that for diastolic, which is not quite the equivalent of going from 125/75 to 124/74, or what the authors described as "not enough to expect an important health benefit." The same authors also noted the difficulty of maintaining a bland, low-salt diet. Several studies have shown no link between limiting salt intake and a lowering the risk of heart attack, stroke, or death. Meanwhile, a variety of studies have found low salt intake is linked to elevated levels of LDL cholesterol and triglycerides, and increased rates of heart disease, heart failure, insulin resistance, and type 2 diabetes.[2] However, there is a link between increased salt intake and stomach cancer (Wang, Terry, and Yan 2009).

The "scientific" evidence of the danger of salt goes back to studies in the 1960s and '70s by Lewis Dahl of the Brookhaven National Laboratory, which showed salt

---

[1]   "Most People Consume Too Much Salt," see under section "Guidelines and Dietary Reference Intakes (DRIs) for Sodium," Centers for Disease Control and Prevention, last reviewed February 26, 2021, https://www.cdc.gov/salt/.

[2]   A summary of these studies can be found in: Hrefna Palsdottir, "Salt: Good or Bad?" Healthline, June 18, 2017, https://www.healthline.com/nutrition/salt-good-or-bad.

caused hypertension in rats when they were fed the equivalent of 500 g a day for humans (i.e., almost 60 times the current average consumption). In 2011, in an article titled "It's Time to End the War on Salt," author Melinda Moyer noted studies that showed,

> *The population that ate the most salt . . . had a lower median blood pressure than the population that ate the least.*
>
> *. . . [A 2006 study] found that the more sodium people ate, the less likely they were to die of heart disease. And a 2007 study . . . found no association between urinary sodium levels and the risk of coronary vascular disease or death."*

The author went on to conclude,

> *For every study that suggests that salt is unhealthy, another does not.* ("It's Time to End the War on Salt," *Scientific American*, July 8, 2011)

Some people do unequivocally experience blood pressure spikes after eating high levels of salt, and almost the same number of people experience drops in blood pressure. Many people see no change. There is no hard and fast rule. Individual sensitivity to salt appears to be tremendously variable, so, in the end, your personal biological sensitivity to salt needs to determine your approach.

It is also possible that high sodium consumption is correlated to other unhealthy factors or habits. The CDC (https://www.cdc.gov/salt/) notes that more than 70% of the sodium consumed by Americans comes from processed food and restaurant meals. These foods, which are also high in sugar and fat, are tied to a host of additional health issues that plague our modern society.

No matter what you think of the long-held wisdom of limiting salt, the general principle of moderation is always a good guide. Maybe, rather than focusing on salt, we should be focusing on eating real food. It could well be the secret of the "French paradox," whereby the population in France has a lower level of coronary heart disease despite a relatively high-fat diet (Ferrières 2004). A big plate of cheese and charcuterie can be an occasional delight. It probably shouldn't be an everyday treat. However, a bowl of rice or other grain with fresh and pickled vegetables is a staple in many countries and the addition of a fried or poached egg makes a complete, delicious meal.

SALT COD

Salt cod is a delicious way to preserve and intensify meaty cod fillets. Even after the fish is soaked to remove salt, the process yields a fillet that is denser than a fresh cod fillet and holds up better in cooking, though it does not strictly have to be cooked since it has already been dry cured. Salt cod is excellent stewed in onions, peppers, and tomatoes; mixed with potatoes, butter, and garlic for fritters or the French brandade; or cooked with peppers, capers, tomato, and potatoes. Traditional recipes for salt cod come from almost every country on the Atlantic, from Norway to Spain and Portugal to the Caribbean and Brazil.

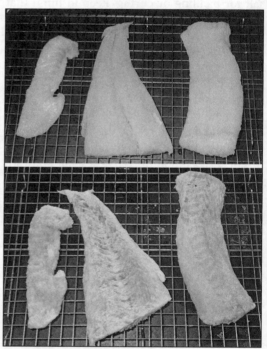

After salting, cod will dry out to a firm, shelf-stable condition (*bottom*).

Salt Cod

Ingredients
- ○ 1 bone-out fillet of cod, about 900 g (~2 lb.)
- ○ 864 g (3 cups) of unrefined salt (While I emphasize in this book the importance of precise measurements, the goal here is to simply bury the cod in salt.)

Directions
1. Break the cod fillet down into manageable pieces, no larger than 20–25 cm (8–10") long. Pack the cod and salt in a large plastic ziplock bag, making sure to distribute the salt across the entire surface of the fillet. Let rest in the fridge for at least two days, taking it out after one day to make sure salt is still covering the entire piece of fish. Moisture will leach out of the fish while it sits, so it is important to check that the fillet pieces maintain contact with either brine or salt crystals. If your fillet loses so much moisture in the first day that this is an issue, you can pour the brine off and add more salt back in.

2. After two days in salt, pull the cod out, rinse, and pat dry. Place a pan with a wire rack in the fridge and put the cod on the rack to dry for at least a week, occasionally pulling out the pan to drain any moisture that accumulates. The cod is ready when it is very dry and stiff. (Do not be afraid to go longer if the fillet is still a little moist or tender. Just as you will not oversalt salted cod, you also will not overdry it.)

3. Salt cod will stay good long enough for a transatlantic voyage by boat, or in the fridge for several months. When you are ready to use it, soak the fillet in at least four changes of water over two days.

Salt Cod

© Getty/nataliaspb

APPENDIX B

EQUIPMENT

In general, a well-stocked kitchen that has knives, mixing bowls, at least one large cutting board, and a few other standard items will be enable you to make most of the recipes in this book. Measuring spoons and cups, accurate scales, at least one kitchen timer, and plastic wrap are essential in an active kitchen. Knives should include a serrated bread knife to cut through crusty bread quickly and cleanly, and a small, very sharp knife or razor to score bread.

Glass canning jars of various sizes are a go-to for pickled vegetables and similar products. They are also good containers for kombucha or yogurt. Over the years I have collected several half-gallon (~2 L) pickle jars that work well for large batches of fermented vegetables. Ceramic crocks are handy for ferments like sauerkraut or kimchi. In most cases, containers need to be glass, ceramic, plastic, or stainless steel. Cheap metal bowls or pots may be reactive and acidic solutions can eat away at them—they are not recommended. Cast iron should also be avoided, although an enameled Dutch oven is an excellent pot for cheesemaking because it retains heat so well and is nonreactive.

Plastic lids for canning jars are available separately, as are the traditional two-piece metal lids. The metal lids are reusable but will eventually degrade. Do not hesitate to toss a lid that has spots where the finish has worn away. There are also lids that have a hole and rubber grommet for an airlock, and vacuum-sealing lids that pull the air out of the jar. Crocks are available with water-seal systems that help maintain a closed environment. There are also plastic lids that have a built-in airlock that fits on standard glass canning jars (i.e., Mason or Ball jars).

Stones sized for your crock will help to weigh down your fermenting veggies, and there are **tempered glass inserts** sized for both wide-mouth and regular mason jars. A wooden tamper is also helpful for pounding kraut or kimchi. **Cotton kitchen twine** is necessary for tying off sausages and useful for tying and hanging soft cheeses to drain. **Cheesecloth and muslin** can be helpful for covering jars or hanging cheese to drain.

pH strips will help to monitor how your acidifying fermentations are proceeding. The advanced homebrewer may even have a **pH meter** in their arsenal already. If not, a decent one can be purchased for about US$50. Be sure it comes with calibration solutions or purchase them along with your meter and follow the calibration instructions that come with your pH meter. A good pH meter that isn't calibrated is not really giving you useful or accurate information.

An **instant-read thermometer** is handy for cooking fermented sausages and cheesemaking, while an **oven thermometer** will help to ensure that you are baking at the target temperature. For salsas and sauces, you might want a strainer or chinois, but this is a matter of personal preference. I tend to just blend thoroughly and do not mind a little rustic texture.

As noted in other chapters, **scales** are necessary because being able to weigh ingredients is important for accuracy and consistency. I have three scales at home. The most frequently used one is a standard kitchen scale that measures up to 5,000 g in one-gram increments, while I also have one for small amounts of yeast or spices that measures up to 100 g in one-hundredth-gram increments. Finally, I have a postage scale that measures up to 16 kg in one-gram increments, which I use for tracking the progress of dry-cured meats.

A **spice grinder/coffee grinder** is great to break down whole spices. (If you are grinding both coffee and spices, just buy a second grinder. You do not need your spices to taste like coffee.) You could also use a mortar and pestle for a more hands-on approach.

What follows is a list of additional equipment useful or recommended for different fermentations.

Baguette pan: A perforated pan with shaped, divided sections that contains your baguette loaves as they cook. Not necessary, but a great tool to help give your baguettes a great, even crust.

Baker's couche or linen: An untreated piece of linen, used to support shaped pieces of dough during the final rise.

Baking stone: Great for retaining heat during baking. Highly recommended for elongated breads (e.g., boules, baguettes) that cannot be cooked in a Dutch oven, and for pizzas.

Bench scraper/dough cutter: A flat piece of steel, a bench scraper helps to cleanly scrape or move a batch of dough onto or off of a cutting board and is used to cleanly divide a batch of dough before preshaping.

Butter muslin: A more fine-mesh cheesecloth, good for draining yogurt or small-curd cheeses. Note that not all suppliers label fine-mesh cheesecloth as muslin.

Cabbage shredder: See mandoline.

Cheesecloth: A woven cotton cloth that comes in different levels of mesh. Fine cheesecloth can be used to drain cheese curds or dairy products such as yogurt. See also butter muslin.

Cheese mold and follower: A molded piece of plastic used to shape your batch of cheese (often round if sold with a follower). When pressing cheeses with weight to expel additional whey, a cheese mold can be paired with a follower, which is fitted to the mold and will even out the distribution of weight.

Cooling rack: Important to use with freshly baked bread, allowing it to cool evenly when it first comes out of the oven. Hot bread needs to rest and finish cooking internally; storing on a flat surface like a cutting board will steam the bottom of the loaf.

Crock: Made of non-reactive, non-porous ceramic, crocks are wider than most jars and straight-sided, ideal for large batches of dry-brined vegetables such as sauerkraut.

Curing chamber: A small dorm-style or mini-fridge is most commonly used in conjunction with a temperature controller. Humidity control can be as simple as cracking the door or putting a pan of salted water in the bottom of the fridge, or as involved as running a humidifier and/or dehumidifier through a programmable humidistat. Not required for the small pieces of dry-cured meat featured in this book, but necessary for curing larger pieces of meat. Also helpful for aging cheeses.

Cut-resistant gloves: Generally made of woven Kevlar fibers. Should be worn whenever using a mandoline or slaw board.

Food-grade plastic tubs: Not necessary for breadmaking, but very helpful to keep track of how your bread is rising.

Humidistat/humidity controller: A programmable humidity controller for a closed system such as a curing chamber.

Mandoline: A slicer with a razor-sharp blade. Must be used with either the supplied safety guard or cut-resistant gloves.

Meat grinder: You could talk to your local butcher about grinding meat for you, but having your own meat grinder opens up a world of opportunities. Grinders can be manual hand-cranked machines, or much faster electric versions. They often come with sausage stuffing attachments for the beginner sausage maker.

Pizza peel: Not just for pizzas, a peel is handy for anything going onto or coming off of your baking stone.

Proofing basket: Also known as a *banneton*, a proofing basket will help contain your shaped dough and imprint a nice pattern into the final loaf.

Sausage stuffer: A dedicated piece of equipment used to stuff sausage, as compared to a dual-purpose meat grinder/sausage stuffer. It is one more piece of equipment, but it cases sausage better than a dual-purpose grinder/stuffer. If you are making a lot of sausage or large batches, it can be worth the investment.

Slaw board: See mandoline.

Thermostat/temperature controller: A programmable temperature controller for a closed system such as a curing chamber.

Weights: Usually made of tempered glass or non-reactive stone, used to weigh down fermenting vegetables below the level of brine in a jar or crock.

RECOMMENDED READING

GENERAL
On Food and Cooking
by Harold McGee

This book remains as essential now as when it was first published in 1984. A groundbreaking examination of the scientific minutiae that underpin our ingredients and the processes our food undergoes, it has opened the eyes of countless cooks and chefs to the chemistry of food.

The Art of Fermentation
by Sandor Katz

This book is as close to an encyclopedic reference as exists for fermented foods. It is an in-depth examination of fermentation and preservation methods used around the world, providing an excellent view of the underlying principles at work in various types of fermentation.

The Noma Guide to Fermentation
by Rene Redzepi and David Zilber

This book is focused much more narrowly on a few specific types of fermentation, including fermented fruits, kombucha, and vinegar, but those familiar with Redzepi's work should not be surprised by the unorthodox recipes and approaches. It is a fantastic view into the creative minds at a groundbreaking restaurant, and a great source of inspiration for those wanting want to push the limits with fermented foods.

BREAD

Bread: A Baker's Book of Techniques and Recipes
by Jeffrey Hamelman

A comprehensive work by a master baker, Hamelman's Bread stretches to nearly 500 pages and touches on virtually every aspect of breadmaking, both technical and practical. Clear, thorough, and in-depth, if you have room for only one bread book on your shelf, this is it.

Peter Reinhart's Artisan Breads Every Day
by Peter Reinhart

This is a great guide to adapting breadmaking to your daily schedule from a great baker and author. You can make a variety of breads, both with baker's yeast and sourdough, on a flexible schedule that can be made to fit your daily routine.

VEGETABLES

Fermented Vegetables
by Kirsten and Christopher Shockey

A great overview of fermented veggies, this book provides plenty of information on topics from equipment and microbiology to principles and recipes for a variety of vegetables. Pickles, krauts and kimchis, pepper and garlic sauces, and a whole gamut of other vegetables are included here.

CHEESE AND DAIRY

Home Cheese Making
by Ricki Carroll

First published in 1982 and revised twice since then, Home Cheese Making hearkens back to the early days of America's artisanal cheese movement. Carroll's book has been the gateway text for generations of home cheesemakers since then, and is still required reading for those hoping to learn the craft.

CHARCUTERIE

Charcuterie: The Craft of Salting, Smoking, and Curing
by Michael Ruhlman and Brian Polcyn

There are a lot of books about home charcuterie on the market these days, but this was the original and remains a fundamental work, required reading for anyone who wants to dive into that world. It also contains amazing chapter titles, such as the poetic ode on sausage: "The Power and the Glory: Animal Fat, Salt, and the Pig Come Together in one of the Oldest, Divine-Yet-Humble Culinary Creations Known to Humankind." The authors are unabashed about a subject that is obviously close to their hearts, and it reflects in the material.

The Art of Making Fermented Sausages
by Stanley and Adam Marianski

The Marianskis have written a variety of books on meat, sausages, curing, and smoking. They provide detailed expertise on the production and safety of fermented sausages in this book, which is a great place to start for those looking to dive deeper into fermented meats.

VINEGAR

Homebrewed Vinegar: How to Ferment 60 Delicious Varieties, Including Carrot-Ginger, Beet, Brown Banana, Pineapple, Corncob, Honey, and Apple Cider Vinegar

by Kirsten Shockey

This book, released after *The Fermentation Kitchen* was written, is a thorough, top-to-bottom approach to vinegar. It tackles the history and science of vinegar, and Shockey takes a deep dive into the wide varieties of vinegar that the home producer can make. Whether using beer, wine, or cider, fruit juice, or even kitchen scraps, she shows that the potential avenues for flavor creation are endless.

Vinegar Revival Cookbook

by Harry Rosenblum

Author and cooking school founder Harry Rosenblum includes a number of recipes for different vinegars, as well as recipes and suggestions to incorporate vinegar into your everyday life. Homemade vinegar can go into cocktails, meals, and be used as a base for homemade pickles.

KOMBUCHA

The Big Book of Kombucha

by Hannah Crum and Alex LaGory

With their comprehensive guide to kombucha, Crum and LaGory provide information on techniques for making kombucha, recipe ideas, and ways to use kombucha beyond just drinking it. They also explore some of the research and gaps in research surrounding kombucha and health.

BIBLIOGRAPHY

Abo, Barbara, Josh Bevan, Surine Greenway, Beverly Healy, Sandra M. McCurdy, Joey Peutz, and Grace Wittman. 2014. "Acidification of Garlic and Herbs for Consumer Preparation of Infused Oils." *Food Protection Trends* 34(4): 247–257.

Bertolli, Paul. 2003. *Cooking by Hand*. New York: Clarkson Potter.

Billing, Jennifer, and Paul W. Sherman. 1998. "Antimicrobial Functions of Spices: Why Some Like It Hot." *Quarterly Review of Biology* 73(1): 3–49. https://doi.org/10.1086/420058.

Boetticher, Taylor, and Toponia Miller. 2013. *In the Charcuterie*. New York: Ten Speed Press.

Carroll, Ricki. 2002. *Home Cheese Making*. 3rd ed. North Adams, MA: Storey Publishing.

Chun, Lauryn. 2012. *The Kimchi Cookbook*. New York: Ten Speed Press.

Crum, Hannah, and Alex LaGory. 2016. *The Big Book of Kombucha: Brewing, Flavoring, and Enjoying the Health Benefits of Fermented Tea*. North Adams, MA: Storey Publishing.

Eschliman, Dwight, and Steve Ettlinger. 2015. *Ingredients: A Visual Exploration of 75 Additives and 25 Food Products*. New York: Regan Arts.

Ferrières, Jean. 2004. "The French Paradox: Lessons for Other Countries." *Heart* 90(1): 107–111. https://doi.org/10.1136/heart.90.1.107.

Forkish, Ken. 2012. *Flour, Water, Salt, Yeast: The Fundamentals of Artisan Bread and Pizza*. New York: Ten Speed Press.

Gottardi, Davide, Danka Bukvicki, Sahdeo Prasad, and Amit K. Tyagi. 2016. "Beneficial Effects of Spices in Food Preservation and Safety." *Frontiers in Microbiology* 7 (September 21): Article 1394. https://doi.org/10.3389/fmicb.2016.01394.

Hamelman, Jeffrey. 2013. *Bread: A Baker's Book of Techniques and Recipes*. 2nd ed. Hoboken, NJ: Wiley.

Hertzberg, Jeff, Zoë François, and Stephen Scott Gross. 2013. *The New Artisan Bread in Five Minutes a Day: the Discovery That Revolutionizes Home Baking*. New York : Thomas Dunne Books/St. Martin's Press.

Kapp, Julie, and Walton Sumner. 2019. "Kombucha: A Systematic Review of the Empirical Evidence of Human Health Benefits." *Annals of Epidemiology* 30:66–70. https://doi.org/10.1016/j.annepidem.2018.11.001.

Karlin, Mary. 2011. *Artisan Cheese Making at Home: Techniques and Recipes for Mastering World-Class Cheeses*. Berkeley: Ten Speed Press.

Katz, Sandor Ellix. 2003. *Wild Fermentation*. White River Junction, VT: Chelsea Green Publishing.

—— 2012. *The Art of Fermentation*. White River Junction, VT: Chelsea Green Publishing.

Kurlansky, Mark. 2002. *Salt: A World History*, New York, NY: Penguin Books.

Lee, Edward. 2013. *Smoke and Pickles*. New York: Artisan.

Marianski, Stanley, and Adam Marianski. 2008. *The Art of Making Fermented Sausages*. Denver: Outskirts Press.

McGee, Harold. 2004. *On Food and Cooking: The Science and Lore of the Kitchen*. Rev. ed. New York: Scribner.

Pollan, Michael. 2013. *Cooked: A Natural History of Transformation*. New York: Penguin Books.

Redzepi, Rene, and David Zilber. 2018. *The Noma Guide to Fermentation*. New York: Artisan.

Reinhart, Peter. 2009. *Peter Reinhart's Artisan Breads Every Day*. New York: Ten Speed Press.

Rosenblum, Harry. 2017. *Vinegar Revival Cookbook: Artisanal Recipes for Brightening Dishes and Drinks with Homemade Vinegars*. New York: Clarkson Potter.

Ruhlman, Michael, and Brian Polcyn. 2005. *Charcuterie: The Craft of Salting, Smoking, and Curing*. New York: W.W. Norton.

Ruhlman, Michael, and Brian Polcyn. 2012. *Salumi: The Craft of Italian Dry Curing*. New York: W.W. Norton.

Shockey, Kirsten, and Christopher Shockey. 2014. *Fermented Vegetables*. North Adams, MA: Storey Publishing.

Shockey, Kirsten, and Christopher Shockey. 2017. *Fiery Ferments*. North Adams, MA: Storey Publishing.

Tsuji, Shizuo. 2011. *Japanese Cooking: A Simple Art*. Rev. ed. New York: Kodansha International.

Wang, Xiao-Qin, Paul D. Terry, and Hong Yan. 2009. "Review of salt consumption and stomach cancer risk: Epidemiological and biological evidence." *World Journal of Gastroenterology* 15(18): 2204–2213. https://doi.org/10.3748/wjg.15.2204.

INDEX